Rumanian Aces of World War 2

SERIES EDITOR: TONY HOLMES

OSPREY AIRCRAFT OF THE ACES® • 54

Rumanian Aces of World War 2

Dénes Bernád

OSPREY
PUBLISHING

Front Cover
On 6 June 1944, *Locotenent aviator* Ion Dobran of the élite *Escadrila 48 vânătoare, Grupul 9 vânătoare*, flying his Bf 109G-6 'Yellow 22', surprised two USAAF P-51Cs of the 317th FS/325th FG flying at high altitude towards Russia. In the ensuing battle, he successfully attacked Mustang 42-103519, flown by six-kill ace 2Lt Barrie Davis, but was forced by the other (42-103501, flown by 11-kill ace 1Lt Wayne Lowry) to land after a chase from 20,000 ft down to ground level. The Rumanian pilot survived the crash landing, but his *Gustav* needed extensive repairs. Due to a lack of witnesses, Dobran's ninth aerial victory remained a probable – 2Lt Davis struggled on to Mirgorod, in the Ukraine, where he successfully landed his Mustang, minus its canopy and with its tail half shot off. Dobran finished the war with 15 victories, ranking him 23rd in the unofficial list of ARR (Rumanian air force) aces. The following edited description of the action is taken from his wartime diary;

'I spot two red-nosed aeroplanes flying at my left, slightly below me. Could they be Me 109Gs of *Escadrila 56*? No, they are American Mustangs. Finally, the moment I have been waiting for! I carefully scout the area behind me. I am alone. I know that one against four means almost certain suicide. Nevertheless, I attack. I see the target growing in my gunsight. Now! Simultaneously, I press the cannon button with my thumb and the machine gun trigger with my index finger. Fire streams erupt from my cowling and spinner. I correct the aim slightly with the help of tracer bullets. At first, the American does not seem to react. Then, hit in the fuselage, he slides underneath the other aircraft. Instinctively looking behind, I spot the other Mustangs approaching. I take the classical escape method – a dive, then recovery. The three Mustangs are stuck to my tail. Only one is dangerously close. Apparently he has greater speed and climbs better. He keeps sticking to my tail, no matter what I do. I try another sudden climb, then like a giant hammer, the first hits. Others follow, without exploding. I spot a thin white stream on the left side of the fuselage. Instinctively, I reduce engine revolutions, intending to bale out, but decide to put my crippled machine down anywhere. I lower my undercarriage and land on unknown terrain. The ground is soft, slowing me abruptly. Fearing the American might strafe, I jump out and look up. I cannot see anything. Only the dying roar of an engine can be faintly heard departing eastwards' (*cover artwork by Mark Postlethwaite*)

First published in Great Britain in 2003 by Osprey Publishing
Elms Court, Chapel Way, Botley, Oxford, OX2 9LP

© 2003 Osprey Publishing Limited

ISBN 1 84176 535 X

Edited by Tony Holmes and Bruce Hales-Dutton
Page design by Tony Truscott
Cover Artwork by Mark Postlethwaite
Aircraft Profiles by John Weal
Index by Bob Munro
Printed by Stamford Press PTE, Singapore

EDITOR'S NOTE
To make this best-selling series as authoritative as possible, the Editor would be interested in hearing from any individual who may have relevant photographs, documentation or first-hand experiences relating to the world's elite pilots, and their aircraft, of the various theatres of war. Any material used will be credited to its original source. Please contact Tony Holmes via e-mail at: tony.holmes@osprey-jets.freeserve.co.uk

For a catalogue of all Osprey Publishing titles please contact us at:

Osprey Direct UK, PO Box 140, Wellingborough, Northants NN8 2FA, UK
E-mail: **info@ospreydirect.co.uk**

Osprey Direct USA, c/o MBI Publishing, 729 Prospect Ave, PO Box 1, Osceola, WI 54020, USA
E-mail: **info@ospreydirectusa.com**

Back Cover
Bf 109E-7 'Yellow 47' (Wk-Nr. 2643) of *Lt av* Ion Galea of *Grupul 5 vânatoare*. Note the three small white victory bars on the fin. See the commentary for Colour Plate 22 for full details pertaining to this aircraft

CONTENTS

INTRODUCTION
AND ACKNOWLEDGEMENTS

Writing about the exploits of Rumanian fighter pilots in World War 2 has been both an honour and a challenge. Presenting to an English-speaking audience the little-known deeds of the *vânātori* – the Rumanian fighter pilots – is long overdue. The results achieved by these outstanding men are indeed noteworthy. They claimed over 1200 aircraft destroyed in the air and on the ground, and even if all of these claims cannot be verified, they were achieved by a small number of pilots. The price paid in return was over 100 fighter pilots killed, yet their achievements are comparable with the best of their adversaries'. And the Rumanians did face the toughest enemies. First, there was the Red Air Force, which by 1944 had grown into a formidable force. Then there was the USAAF, and finally, and perhaps most deadly of all, the Luftwaffe.

The airmen of the ARR (the Royal Rumanian Air Force), often flying obsolescent aircraft and from 1943 onwards technically inferior to the enemy's and usually fewer in numbers, fought these tough enemies with the same *élan*, gallantry and determination as their Allied counterparts. Almost 60 years after the war, it can be openly said that although for most of their careers they were on the losing side, the Rumanians – and pilots of the other smaller Axis air forces – cannot be considered morally inferior to their Allied counterparts. They fought with devotion for the cause they believed in – their homeland. They flew, and occasionally died, in their aircraft just as their adversaries did – with commitment, and sometimes fearful of imminent danger. This fact deserves unconditional respect, regardless of what is taught in schools or what is often erroneously considered 'political correctness'.

Obtaining a clear picture of the actions and achievements of the Rumanian fighter pilots was not easy. During more than 40 years under an oppressive Communist régime, Rumania's participation in the war against the Soviets was officially ignored. History books started on the night of 23 August 1944, when Rumania defected from the Axis camp and unilaterally joined the Allies. Most former pilots I interviewed during that dark period were at first reluctant to talk about their experiences on the eastern front. Some even refused. Sometimes my status as a member of the Hungarian ethnic minority did not help either. Nevertheless, after I had gained their confidence they began to reveal the stories of how they had fought the Soviets or the Americans.

Before actually meeting these veterans, whose names were well known within a restricted circle, I imagined them as tall, muscular figures with commanding voices, confident of their 'fighter' status. However, most proved to be rather small, thinly-built, frail old men who constantly brushed aside their 'larger-than-life' status. Rather than boosting their own individual successes and adventures, they often

The pilot of an ARR Bf 109G waggles his wings victoriously after a successful combat sortie on the eastern front in the spring of 1944. Seated around the table are, from right to left, *Cpt av* Alexandru Sarbănescu (the second ranking Rumanian ace with 55 victories), *Of ech cl III* Ioan Milu (the third ranking ace with 52 victories), *Adj av* Ioan Mucenica (the eighth ranking ace with 27 victories) and *Lt av* Hariton Dusescu (39th in the unofficial list of ARR aces with 12 victories). In four years of war, Rumanian fighter pilots claimed an estimated 1200 enemy aircraft destroyed in aerial combat or on the ground, which was the equivalent of approximately 1800 victories under the ARR's unique scoring system. In turn, the *vânători* lost more than 100 of their number in combat

showed their true character by directing attention to the sacrifices of former comrades who had lost their lives in the line of duty.

After the fall of Communism in December 1989 things changed, but I had left the country by then. Since 1992, I have returned every year to study the Rumanian archives, which are now open to a limited number of researchers. Now, after almost 20 years of unearthing, then piecing together the vital official information, I can state that the overall picture is fairly clear, and the time for a book about the *vânători* is ripe. But it is also a fact that the complete story cannot, and probably will not, ever be told.

With an estimated 95 per cent of all ARR victory claims processed in my database, I could draw up a tentative list of those pilots we glamorously call 'aces'. This 'master' list is the first serious and systematic attempt to compile a comprehensive register of Rumanian fighter pilots who scored at least five ARR victories. It should be noted, however – as detailed in the appendices – that according to ARR standards, a pilot was credited with *one or more* victories for an enemy aircraft downed in air combat or destroyed on the ground depending on the number of engines it had. As this atypical method of counting victories was the official standard, it is used throughout this book.

Due to the size of this publication, the amount of information which could be included on the *vânători*, and their aircraft, has, by necessity, been restricted. Nevertheless, I sincerely hope I have succeeded in presenting a fair and objective account of the Rumanian fighter pilots' achievements, successes and failures, victories and losses.

To all these men, who sacrificed their lives on the altar of their devotion and duty to their country, regardless of the colours their fighters wore, I express my utmost admiration and respect.

I would particularly like to thank Dan Antoniu and George Cicos from Bucharest for their invaluable help in compiling the 'master' list of 'aces'. The following veterans, colleagues and friends also offered assistance (in alphabetical order) – Mihai Andrei, Valeriu Avram, Ion Becherete, Răzvan Bujor, Ioan Di Cesare, Ion Dobran, Ion Galea (deceased), Vasile Gavriliu (deceased), Teodor Greceanu (deceased), Dmitriy Karlenko, Ovidiu George Man, Cornel Marandiuc, Mihai Moisescu, Cornel Năstase, Victor Nitu, Horia Pop (deceased), Jean-Louis Roba and Ion Tarălungă (deceased). The staff at *Arhivele Militare Române* in Bucharest greatly assisted my researches as well.

Most of the photographs in this book come from the author's personal collection, as well as those of Dan Antoniu and Constantin Bujor. Other contributors were (in alphabetical order) – Valeriu Avram, Cristian Crăciunoiu, Ferdinando D'Amico, Ion Galea, Teodor Greceanu, Mihai Moisescu and Peter Petrick. Several photographs came from the official archives of BA, ECPA, MMN and SMP as well.

I dedicate this book to my parents, Bernád Dénes Sr and Bernád Katalin-Margit, who always encouraged me not to give up pursuing my dreams.

Dénes Bernád
Toronto,
February 2003

BACKGROUND TO WAR

Between the two World Wars, the Kingdom of Rumania was the most powerful and influential state in Eastern Europe and the Balkans. In that most volatile region it fielded the largest army, air force and navy, although it remained under the shadow of the Soviet Union. However, by the late 1930s Rumania was becoming increasingly threatened by some of its neighbours, particularly the USSR, Hungary and Bulgaria, which all sought to recover territories lost two decades earlier. Only countries created after World War 1, such as Poland, Czechoslovakia and Yugoslavia, which bordered Rumania to the north and south-west, could be considered friendly.

Despite its strength on paper, the combat efficiency of *Aeronautica Regală Română* (ARR, or the Royal Rumanian Air Force) was less than adequate. The large number of aircraft types, along with a similarly wide variety of powerplants, created a maintenance nightmare. The result was low aircraft availability, making the numerically large ARR an inefficient and obsolescent air force when compared with the emerging trends in Europe, where many countries were re-arming.

In the 1930s increasing tension in Europe threatened the very existence of the so-called 'Greater Rumania', which had been created in the aftermath of World War 1. ARR headquarters finally decided to act, and a restructuring programme was ordered in June 1936.

As the first stage, obsolescent French and Polish types were to be replaced by 406 new aircraft – 60 reconnaissance, 132 observation and army co-operation machines, 150 fighters and 64 bombers. This would be enough to equip 36 new *escadrile* (squadrons) within the following two-and-half years. The second stage envisaged the purchase of a further 169 aircraft – 105 of which would be fighters – to create 13 new squadrons. These measures were to be implemented between 1 January 1939 and 1 April 1942. The third step called for another 96 aircraft to enter service by 1 April 1944. No further fighters were considered necessary for that period, although losses through attrition would be made good. Due to the precarious state of the indigenous aviation industry, most new aircraft would be purchased from abroad.

In April 1939, in pursuit of its ambitious plans, Rumania sent a substantial military delegation on a round of visits to armament factories in France and the United Kingdom, as well as Germany. The Rumanians returned with a shopping basket full of firm orders and promised deliveries. Fifty Hurricane Mk Is were ordered from Great Britain, with 12 for urgent delivery, while 30 'off-the-shelf' He 112Bs were purchased from Germany, with an additional 50 Bf 109Es also promised. But an unpleasant surprise awaited the Rumanians in France. That country, which until then had provided most of the

ARR's inventory, declined to supply significant numbers of fighters because they were badly needed by the *Armée de l'Air*.

On 12 August 1939, the influx of Western-built aircraft meant that the ARR had 121 combat-ready fighters. Besides the Polish gull-winged PZL P.11s and P.24s, which still formed the mainstay of the ARR's fighter force, the inventory also included the first He 112s and Hurricanes. By the following June, when war had been raging in Europe for more than nine months, 122 fighters were among the total of 587 frontline aircraft. This number comprised 30 PZL P.24Es, 30 He 112Bs, 20 Bf 109Es and 12 Hurricanes, together with 30 IAR 80s of indigenous manufacture. However, the latter type had not actually been delivered because the first batch was still undergoing acceptance testing at the factory. So, apart from the latest Bf 109Es, the most noticeable difference compared to the previous year's line-up was that the obsolescent IAR-built PZL P.11B/Fs were no longer listed as being in frontline service. This meant that by mid-1940 all the ARR's main fighter squadrons were equipped with modern equipment.

Compared to neighbouring countries, therefore, Rumania boasted a superior fighter force, but the wide range of aircraft of differing origins still hindered efficiency and reliability. Serviceability and shortage of spare parts remained the ARR's Achilles' heel, constantly reducing the number of serviceable machines by at least 20 to 30 per cent. With the withdrawal of the surviving Polish air force to Rumania in mid-September 1939, the inventory was unexpectedly enlarged by over 250 aircraft, including some 60 PZL fighters. But only about 30 P.11Cs could be considered as having any combat value, with the other Polish fighter types being relegated to training squadrons.

The order for 50 PZL P.11bs placed in 1933 represented a departure from the normal Rumanian policy of procuring fighters from France. This gull-winged Polish aircraft, powered by a French Gnome Le Rhône radial engine, formed the backbone of the ARR's fighter arm for the next five years – a time of rapid technological advance. Here, Luftwaffe personnel – veterans of the Polish Campaign of September 1939 – examine a P.11F painted in their new ally's colours. Note that although the Fleet F-10G trainer and liaison aircraft in the background already wears the new 'Michael's Cross' national markings, the P.11 still displays the pre-war cockades, suggesting that this photograph was taken in early May 1941, when the markings change took place. 'White 136' was seriously damaged during a dogfight with eight I-16s east of the River Dnestr during an early morning combat on 21 August 1941. Despite the damage, its pilot, *Slt av* Mircea Dumitrescu (a future ace with 13 victories) of *Grupul 3 vânătoare*, was able to return to his base at Elsass, in the Trans-Dnestra Region

Hurricane Mk I 'Yellow 1' was usually flown by *Cpt av* Emil Georgescu, CO of the independent *Escadrila 53 vânătoare*. By the end of the ARR's first campaign, Georgescu had been credited with four confirmed and one unconfirmed kills, amounting to eight victories – he did not claim any more victories. Note the mounted 'Mickey Mouse' with lance squadron emblem, inspired by the popular Disney cartoon character

9

INDIGENOUS FIGHTER

From the late 1930s, the Rumanian aircraft industry was also making significant progress, with the IAR works at Brasov achieving notable success. Following the failure to secure an order for its early fighter types, the IAR design team came up with a new fighter project in late 1938. Designated the IAR 80, this was based partly on knowledge gained from licence production of the Polish PZL P.24 fighter and the Italian Savoia-Marchetti SM.79B bomber. Powered by a French radial engine spinning a German propeller, the new design incorporated modern features like low-wing monoplane configuration, all-metal structure and a retractable undercarriage. Yet the aircraft retained an open cockpit, lacked radio equipment and was armed with no more than a pair of rifle-calibre 7.92 mm wing-mounted machine guns.

Nevertheless, when first flown in April 1939, the IAR 80 surpassed all expectations, and in December 1939 the Ministry of Air and Navy ordered 100. A similar order for the second batch of improved IAR 80As came the following August, but the first 20 early-series IAR 80s were not delivered until February 1941. This was due to a range of problems, including material shortages, delays in armament availability, undercarriage failures and engine unreliability. Initial deliveries were made to the *Flotila 2 vânătoare* (2nd Fighter Flotilla) and the new aircraft equipped *Escadrile* 59 and 60 *vânătoare* (59th and 60th Fighter Squadrons) of the newly created *Grupul 8 vânătoare* (8th Fighter Group). The next batch of 30 arrived at Târgsor in April.

Parallel deliveries of Bf 109Es were also being made, and by the spring of 1941 the remaining 30 on order had been accepted by the élite *Grupul 7 vânătoare*, formed on 1 June 1940 with Hurricanes and Bf 109Es. The newly-arrived machines took the available ARR fighter strength to a peak of 200+ frontline aircraft. This was just in time, as Rumania was about to go to war with the Soviet Union.

TURBULENT TIMES

At the outbreak of World War 2, Rumania was ruled by King Carol (Charles) II. He had seized the throne in 1930, and embraced an increasingly authoritarian style of leadership modelled on that of

A pair of IAR 80s patrol the Bessarabian sky in the summer of 1941. Closest to the camera in 'White 82' is *Slt av* Arghir Borcescu, who claimed two victories prior to being killed in a flying accident on 2 October 1941. His wingman is *Adj stag av* Dumitru Borcescu, who also claimed two victories. Both served with *Grupul 8 vânătoare*. Note that the engine cowlings on both machines are painted in camouflage colours instead of the usual Axis yellow, and that each aircraft has a different style of 'Michael's Cross' national marking

Italian dictator Benito Mussolini. Territorial losses to the USSR, Hungary and Bulgaria in 1940, along with his increasing unpopularity, forced the King to abdicate in favour of his 18-year-old son Mihai (Michael) on 6 September 1940. With the abdication of the King, real power in Rumania passed to the pro-German General, later Marshal, Ion Antonescu, who was declared *conducător*, or 'leader' (i.e. dictator) that same day. Now events moved swiftly. Ten days after Antonescu assumed power, the pro-Nazi 'Iron Guard' became the country's only recognised political party, and Rumania became a 'National Legionary State'. In early October, the first German troops arrived in Rumania, and the following month Antonescu travelled to Berlin to sign the Tripartite (Axis) Pact. Rumania was now firmly in the Axis camp.

Although the Rumanian Government did not accept Hitler's invitation to participate in the assault on Yugoslavia in April 1941, it allowed Luftwaffe units to launch attacks from Rumanian bases. Then, on 22 June 1941, Rumania declared war on the Soviet Union. The stage was set for tragedy and high drama, which would see Rumania fight on both sides, and then spend 45 years as a satellite of the USSR.

NEW COLOURS

In preparation for the war with the USSR a new national marking – a modified Maltese Cross – was adopted in mid-May 1941. It comprised four white bordered blue 'M's (for King Michael) arranged in the shape of a cross and filled with yellow. A small version of the earlier red-yellow-blue cockade was applied in the centre. In some cases a blue 'I' was also inserted between the legs of the four 'M's to symbolise King Michael I. As a further departure from the previous style, the new markings were applied in six positions, including the fuselage sides, rather than just on wing surfaces. To conform to Luftwaffe regulations, the engine cowlings of all ARR aircraft were painted in the chrome yellow Axis recognition colour. Additionally, like all Axis aircraft operating on the eastern front, a yellow band was also applied to the rear fuselage and undersurface wing tips of both military and civilian types. Sometimes, this band was also applied to upper wing tips of certain Rumanian types.

The earlier olive green/light blue camouflage scheme was retained, although from early 1941 large burned-out earth brown (*terra cotta*), and occasionally dark green, wavy stripes were painted above the olive green on the new machines manufactured by IAR Brasov, or purchased from abroad. Exceptions were British and Polish aircraft. They retained the original camouflage schemes, which basically complied with regulations up to the time of their first general overhaul, when standard ARR camouflage was applied.

Each aircraft received an individual serial number, applied in white (sometimes in yellow or red) on the fin rather than on fuselage sides as before. The sole exception was that German-built fighters had their serial numbers on the fuselage, usually between the national markings and the yellow band. There were no mandatory squadron emblems, although some fighter units had their own crests, often inspired by Disney cartoon figures. These new regulations were implemented by early June 1941, just in time for hostilities against the USSR.

11

BARBAROSSA TO STALINGRAD

I n mid-June 1941, the best-equipped fighter groups were placed under the command of *Gruparea Aeriană de Luptă* (GAL or Combat Air Grouping), the main ARR unit designated to support the planned Rumanian and German offensive in the south-western area of the Soviet Union. The fighter groups assigned to GAL were *Grupul 5 vânătoare* (*Escadrile 51* and *52*), with He 112Bs, *Grupul 7 vânătoare* (*Escadrile 56, 57* and *58*), with Bf 109Es, both of these units being part of *Flotila 1 vânătoare*, and *Grupul 8 vânătoare* (*Escadrile 41, 59* and *60*), with its IAR 80s and 80As, part of *Flotila 2 vânătoare*.

On 22 June, GAL listed the following fighters in its inventory (available/unavailable) – 23/1 IAR 80s, 23/5 He 112Bs and 30/6 Bf 109Es, giving a total of 76/12 aircraft.

Interestingly, *Grupul 8 vânătoare*, which was equipped with the indigenous IAR 80, was the only unit assigned a pure fighter role. *Grupul 5 vânătoare* and *Grupul 7 vânătoare*, with their superior German aircraft, were employed primarily as fighter-bombers and bomber escorts. This was probably due to the joint German-Rumanian strategy that saw the crucial fighter role chiefly assigned to the more experienced Luftwaffe *Jagdfliegern*. Additionally, the Hurricane-equipped *Escadrila 53 vânătoare* was transferred temporarily from *Grupul 5 vânătoare* to *Comandamentul Aero Dobrogea* (Air Command Dobruja) and initially assigned the defence of the Black Sea coast, including the vital Constanta harbour and the strategic Cernavodă railway bridge across the Danube.

Alongside the coastal defence Hurricanes, three secondary fighter groups with gull-winged PZLs that were not incorporated into GAL protected the rear front zone and the capital as follows – *Grupul 3*

One of *Grupul 6 vânătoare's* PZL P.24Es is seen parked at Bucharest-Pipera airfield in the summer of 1941. The pilot standing in front of the fighter is believed to be *Adj stag av* Nicolae Solomon (two victories) of *Escadrila 62 vânătoare*, who was killed in action on 18 September 1942 on the Stalingrad front. The aircraft's upper wing surfaces and fuselage are camouflaged in dark green and earth brown, while the undersurfaces are light blue. The white lettering at the fin tip reads *P24 P*, instead of the usual *P24 E*. The reason for this discrepancy remains unknown. Note the Bf 109Es of *Grupul 7 vânătoare* in the background

NCO pilots of *Grupul 6 vânătoare* pose for a group shot in front of a P.24E at Bucharest-Otopeni airfield in the summer of 1941. Included in this group are *Serg TR av* Ioan Olteanu (two victories), *Serg TR rez av* Iosif 'Joshka' Moraru (13 victories) and *Adj stag av* Grigore Mincu (no score). Note the hand-painted yellow fuselage ring – an Axis recognition feature applied to all ARR aircraft in May 1941

An in-flight shot of a PZL P.11F from one of the two fighter groups of *Flotila 3 vânătoare* that were still equipped with the type in the summer of 1941. Powered by a 595 hp radial engine and armed with four 7.92 mm Browning FN machine guns, the P.11F was considered equivalent to the Polikarpov I-15 and I-153 biplanes of the VVS, but inferior to the I-16 monoplane. Among the five fighter types used by the Rumanians at the beginning of the war, the P.11 was certainly the most obsolescent, and accordingly achieved the poorest results in combat

vânătoare (*Escadrile 43, 44* and *45*), equipped with PZL P.11Fs, and *Grupul 4 vânătoare* (*Escadrile 46, 49* and *50*), flying PZL P.11Cs and Fs, were both part of *Flotila 3 vânătoare*, while *Grupul 6 vânătoare* (*Escadrile 61* and *62*), equipped with PZL P.24Es and Ps, served within *Flotila 2 vânătoare*.

On 22 June, the fighter units not incorporated in GAL had ten Hurricanes, 54 P.11s and 20 P.24s available for action. While the Bucharest-Otopeni-based *Grupul 6* was assigned to defend the capital, *Grupuri 3* and *4* flew mainly fighter-bomber missions, dropping small 4.4-lb grenades from under-wing racks. Secondary roles included carrying out area interdiction missions and the interception of aircraft.

At the start of Operation *Barbarossa*, therefore, there were 76 fighters and fighter-bombers available to GAL, with an additional 12 in reserve (35 per cent of GAL's inventory), while 102 PZL fighters were available outside GAL, with another 22 in reserve. Thirteen

Hurricanes completed the list. The overall total of 225 fighters and fighter-bombers represented about 40 per cent of the ARR's combat aircraft inventory.

Some 672 Rumanian aircraft, together with about 420 Luftwaffe machines, faced a numerically superior but qualitatively inferior Red Air Force. The *Voyenno-Vozdushniye Sily* (VVS, or Soviet Air Force) fielded some 950 aircraft subordinated to the Odessa Military District (OdVO, later renamed *Southern Front*), covering the area between Kamenets-Podolskiy and the Danube Delta. This encompassed the whole of Bessarabia (Soviet Moldavia) and adjacent areas of the Ukraine. The 624-strong Black Sea Fleet (ChF) operated in the same area. Finally, some of the 350 bombers belonging to Long-range Bomber Aviation (DBA) were also available for attacks on Rumania. Despite the Soviets' numerical superiority (estimated to be in the ratio of 1.6 to 1), technical superiority belonged to the Axis side, since a much higher proportion of the VVS combat fleet – about three-quarters – was obsolete.

FIRST BLOOD

Combat was particularly fierce on the first day of the offensive (22 June), and the *vânători* acquitted themselves well. They were credited with ten aircraft confirmed as destroyed in the air, plus two probables, and eight on the ground – a total of 23 victories. The Hurricane pilots were particularly successful, being credited with a total of eight aircraft confirmed and one unconfirmed for no loss. At least 11 fighters returned with combat damage or with their engines seized, however, although none were written-off. Two pilots were wounded in action. The IAR 80-equipped patrols achieved only one aerial kill during four separate battles. The victory was claimed by *Sublocotenent aviator* (Pilot Officer) Ioan Mihăilescu of *Esc 60 vân* – a future ace with five victories, all achieved in 1941. However, at least four IAR 80s force-landed with battle damage, whilst another two suffered engine trouble.

The hero among the *vânători* was undoubtedly *Slt av* Teodor Moscu of *Escadrila 51 vânătoare*. Shortly after noon, while strafing Bulgărica airfield in southern Bessarabia, he was engaged by several I-16s. In the ensuing mêlée, Moscu shot down two of his attackers, while a third

The entire complement of *Escadrila 61 vânătoare* gather in front of one of the squadron's PZL P.24Es at Bucharest-Otopeni airfield on 20 August 1941. *Lt C-dor av* Nicolae 'Nae' Rădulescu, CO of *Grupul 6 vânătoare* (parent unit of *Escadrila 61 vânătoare*) stands in the centre of the photo. To his left is *Cpt av* Ioan Cara, squadron CO, who scored one kill over a Yak east of Stalingrad on 14 September 1942. Cara and Rădulescu are in turn flanked by the squadron's three *sublocotenenti aviatori*, Mihail Slăvescu, Leonid Sotropa and Nicolae Niculescu. Note the fighter's light armament – only one pair of 7.92 mm Browning FN machine guns – which was wholly inadequate by 1941 standards remained unconfirmed. His He 112B ('Black 13') was damaged, Moscu being barely able to reach the closest Rumanian airfield to the frontline, Bârlad. This did not signal the start of an outstanding career for *Slt av* Teodor Moscu, however, as no trace has been found of any further victories credited to him.

Two other pilots who scored their first kills on this day were *Adj stag av* (Lance Corporal) Constantin Pomut and *Adj stag av* Petre Cordescu, both from Hurricane-equipped *Escadrila 53*. Each achieved two confirmed aerial victories, and they would subsequently be among the top aces of the first ARR campaign. Indeed, Pomut became the first 'ace-in-a-day', later being credited with two 'Seversky' fighters and one twin-engined seaplane, while the destruction of a second similar machine remained unconfirmed. Under the ARR scoring system, he was credited with six victories (see the Appendix for a full explanation of the ARR scoring system).

There was a temporary lull in combat on 23 June. Nevertheless, fighters were active over the front as well as in home defence, where the best unit was again the Hurricane squadron. Its most successful pilot that day was 30-year-old *Locotenent aviator* (Flying Officer) Horia Agarici, who shot down three Soviet SB bombers of ChF near Constanta harbour. Agarici became an instant hero and celebrity, and by evening the people of Constanta had made him the subject of a song, celebrating him as a 'Bolshevik hunter'. Although his fame continued long after the war, Agarici did not enjoy an outstanding career as an 'ace' fighter pilot.

The Rumanian pilots' luck on the first day was not to last. Four ARR fighters were reported as having been destroyed on 23 June, with three pilots lost. The first to die was *Adjutant aviator* (Corporal) Anghel Codrut of *Grupul 5 vânătoare*, whose He 112B ('Black 12') was set on fire by Soviet fighters over Bolgrad airfield, in southern Bessarabia. Soviet sources credit a He 112 'kill' to *Kapitan* Piotr Kozachenko of 249 IAP, but this claim seems unlikely due to the vast distance between the locations of the two battles, and the Soviet claim is probably the result of faulty aircraft identification.

During the first two weeks of the campaign, the Rumanian fighter pilots' main task continued to be the protection of bombers and reconnaissance aircraft, together with ground attack, although occasional fighter sorties were permitted. During the night of 2/3 July, however, a joint German-Rumanian offensive was launched across the River Prut involving Luftwaffe and ARR fighters in direct support of advancing troops. This was achieved by increasing the number of ground support sorties, with a

Two unidentified black leather-clad *vânători* of *Escadrila 51 vânătoare* search the sky for incoming aircraft. Note the grey-painted He 112s parked behind them among the trees on what is believed to be Salz airfield, near the River Dnestr's eastern banks in the so-called Region of Trans-Dnestra (Transnistria in Rumanian). The contrast between forest green and light grey did not provide an effective camouflage scheme for these aircraft while they were on the ground

Horia Agarici became the darling of the Rumanian people because he was seen as a typical hero in the fight against the feared Soviets. He was cast in this role by wartime propaganda, which exploited his one major success to the fullest extent. In the early morning of the war's second day, *Lt av* Agarici hastily took off in Hurricane 'Yellow 3', which was minus its engine cowling panels, and single-handedly downed all three Soviet bombers attempting to attack Constanta harbour. By the evening, when word of his feat had spread, he had instantly became a national hero. A song was hastily composed in his honour, based on the coincidence that 'Agarici' rhymed with 'bolsevici' (Rumanian for 'Bolshevik', or Soviet), so that the jingle ran, 'Agarici has gone to hunt bolsevici'. It quickly became popular all over Rumania, and although Agarici become an ace with six confirmed kills and two probables, amounting to 13 victories, he failed to achieve any further major successes, sometimes even being reluctant to take up battle with enemy aircraft. And the song was to return to haunt him when the 'bolsevici' became Rumania's masters in late 1944. In this official photograph, Agarici is wearing the Aeronautical Virtue with Swords Order, with two bars (at left), as well as the Charles I Centennial Medal above his pilot's badge

consequent reduction in escort and free hunt missions, and was only made possible by a lack of substantial enemy air activity. Nevertheless, Soviet anti-aircraft gunners were gaining experience and becoming more effective. As Rumanian veteran pilots recall, it was not Soviet fighters but flak which posed the main threat during the entire eastern front campaign.

The battle for Bessarabia reached its peak on 12 July. Between 0850 and 1940 hrs, 59 ARR bombers in nine waves made a non-stop attack on Soviet targets east of the Fălciu bridgehead. Cover was provided by a further 54 fighters. Enemy troops, transport and armoured vehicles were continuously bombed and strafed. As a consequence, the developing Soviet counter-offensive was slowed to a standstill. Several air battles raged between German-Rumanian and Soviet fighters. Unusually, the Soviets appeared in large numbers over a sector of the front, which was regarded by both the Soviets and the Germans – but obviously not by the Rumanians – as of secondary importance.

One of the most noteworthy episodes for ARR personnel was the sacrifice of *Slt av* Vasile Claru of *Grupul 8 vânătoare*. After reportedly shooting down three of the six I-16s he encountered over the battlefield, Claru had run out of ammunition, so he used his IAR 80 ('White 23') to ram one of the enemy fighters above Tiganca. He destroyed it, but paid the ultimate price, although it is not clear if his was a deliberate act, or whether the collision was an accident in the heat of combat. His victim was probably Lt Ilya M Shamanov, deputy commander of one of the 67 IAP's *eskadrily* (squadrons), who was reported to have performed a 'taran' in the same area. The same *polk* (regiment) claimed six enemy aircraft shot down, but only two Rumanian fighters failed to return from combat, including Claru's.

There is no confirmation of Claru's three victories, only a record of the single enemy aircraft destroyed in the collision. Whatever the cause, the incident was quickly hailed by Rumanian propaganda as an example of supreme sacrifice for 'King and Country'.

Another example of courage and devotion to duty was provided by *Lt rez av ing* (Flying Officer in reserve, Dipl Eng) Ioan Lascu of *Grupul 5 vânătoare*. Returning from a combat sortie with his aircraft damaged, Lascu insisted on heading back to the frontline to finish off the remaining targets. His request was approved, and Lascu took off with a replacement He 112B ('Black 1') for the last mission of the day. While strafing an artillery position at Tiganca, his Heinkel was hit by small-arms fire and the pilot mortally wounded. Both Claru and Lascu posthumously received Rumania's military award for officers, the *Mihai Viteazul* (Michael the Brave) Order, Third Class. These decorations were the first awarded to ARR personnel, and only 40 airmen received them during the bloody campaign against the Allies.

Despite the losses, Rumanian fighter pilots achieved at least six aerial victories that day, the IAR 80-equipped *Gr 8 vân* claiming four Soviet fighters, including Claru's. One of the other claimants was *Slt av* Ion Zaharia of *Escadrila 52 vânătoare*. He 'flamed' one of four I-16 *Ratas* that he discovered attacking PZL P.37B '218' in the Lărguta area.

On 26 July the territory between the Prut and Dnestr rivers was secured by Rumanian troops. Bessarabia and northern Bukovina were

Slt rez av Dipl Eng Ioan Lascu of *Escadrila 51 vânătoare* received a head wound in combat during the first days of the war against the USSR. Here, he poses for what was probably one of his last photographs, as he was shot down and killed by Soviet flak at Valea Hârtoapelor, near Tiganca, on 12 July 1941. Lascu had shot down a MiG-3 just 48 hours into the war with the Soviet Union, his victim crash-landing near Lake Balta Albă in Râmnicul Sărat County, Moldavia. Soviet pilot N Viktorov, possibly from 146 IAP, was taken prisoner. Lascu's victory was one of the very few aerial successes credited to the He 112, as the type was primarily assigned to ground attack rather than pure fighter duties, which were reserved for the more experienced Luftwaffe *Jagdfliegern*

After the ARR's 1941 campaign, surviving He 112s served briefly in the coastal patrol role, operating from Odessa until 1 July 1942. Later, the type became a conversion trainer for pilots moving from the IAR 80 to the Bf 109G. This particular aircraft is He 112B-2 'White 30' (Wk-Nr. 2037), which was the last example of the type to enter Rumanian service. It is parked on the snowy runway at Bucharest-Pipera airfield in late 1942. The white 'Edelweiss' motif visible forward of the cockpit was a personal emblem

now considered liberated from Soviet control, and part of the Kingdom of Rumania once more. The goal had been achieved after a month-long battle in which a total of 5100 sorties had been flown by ARR aircraft, the *vânători* accounting for 2162 of them. Rumanian airmen claimed 88 enemy aircraft destroyed in aerial combat, the majority of these falling to fighters. A further 108 had been destroyed on the ground and 59 by flak. Altogether, 58 Rumanian aircraft had been lost in combat, with at least 18 fighter pilots killed in action, in accidents or listed as missing in action.

THE BATTLE FOR ODESSA

Combat did not stop when the Dnestr had been reached and Bessarabia retaken. The next goal was Odessa, the main communications hub and harbour of the Black Sea's north-west coast. But the target was beyond the range of Rumania-based aircraft. To cut flying time and reduce the already overstretched supply lines, most ARR combat units were ordered forward to landing grounds that had previously been used by the VVS, or were newly established in the recently-acquired territory of southern Bessarabia.

Several fighter units also had to be reorganised and restructured. On 13 August, the badly-mauled *Grupul 5 vânătoare* was reduced to just one squadron, the 51st. The 52nd, after handing over its surviving He 112Bs to its sister squadron, was amalgamated with the similarly-battered *Escadrila 42*, equipped with IAR 80s. The mixed squadron, renamed *Escadrila 42/52 vânătoare*, received new IAR 80As and was relegated to the home defence role.

With new forward bases, fighter units also requested additional aircraft to replace losses. The ARR could not, however, rely on replacements from German sources because the Luftwaffe was not then required to make good its allies' losses. This is why the only units to

Due to heavy losses sustained by *Grupul 5 vânătoare* in its ground attack role, personnel from one of the *Grup's* two squadrons (*Escadrila 52 vânătoare*) merged with *Escadrila 42 vânătoare* on 15 July 1941 – the resulting *Esc 42/52 vân* was equipped with new IAR 80As. This shot shows the new unit's entire complement of pilots. They are, from left to right, top row, Prince *Slt av* Mihai Brâncoveanu, *Slt av* Victor Jemna, CO and 1st Patrol leader *Cpt av* Prince Marin Ghica (6+) and *Adj stag av* Dumitru Encioiu (five). Middle row, from left to right, *Slt av* Panait Grigore (nine victories – killed on 5 May 1944), *Slt av* Mihai Lucaci, leader of the 2nd Patrol *Lt rez av* Baron Radu Reinek (six) and *Adj av* Mircea Simion (two). Front row, from left to right, *Serg T R av* Radu Costache (two), *Slt av* Flaviu Zamfirescu (four victories – killed on 22 May 1944), leader of the 3rd Patrol *Of ech cl III av* Ioan Maga (29) and *Adj av* Vladimir Botnar

receive new aircraft were those equipped with the indigenous IAR 80, and several PZL squadrons began conversion onto the type.

The struggle for Odessa opened on 8 August. Gradually, air battles became more frequent, both sides considering the city and harbour to be vital. An impressive number of aerial victories was claimed. For example, during the evening of the renewed Axis offensive, I-16 pilots of 69 IAP reportedly shot down nine out of twelve Bf 109Es encountered above Odessa, yet no Rumanian *Emils* were lost that day, and only two Luftwaffe Bf 109F-4s were damaged by enemy fighters on the entire eastern front! The next day, pilots of the same VVS fighter regiment filed claims for five P.24s out of twenty engaged in a dogfight, while admitting the loss of two of their own aircraft and a third damaged. Five P.11Fs were actually damaged in combat that day, but all were able to return to base. In turn, Rumanian PZL pilots claimed nine *Ratas*.

On the 19th, a further seven Axis aircraft were claimed by 69 IAP, while 9 IAP of the Black Sea Fleet reported eight shot down. Again, few of these claims are matched by corresponding losses on the Axis side. The Rumanians over-claimed as well, but apparently to a lesser degree than the Soviets. On the afternoon of 21 August, over Dalnik, several Bf 109Es of *Grupul 7 vânătoare* clashed with a dozen Ilyushin Il-2s escorted by about 20 Yakovlev Yak-1s. It is believed the Yaks were

either ex-8 IAP machines of the ChF, transferred to 69 IAP just days earlier, or 9 IAP-ChF aircraft, based at Ocheakov, near Nikolaev. At the same time, a quartet of Il-2s from 46 OShAE (*Otdel'naya Shturmovaya Aviatsionnaya Eskadrilya*, Independent Ground Attack Squadron) had also been included in the strength of 69 IAP.

The commanding officer of the élite Messerschmitt-equipped group, *Locotenent comandor aviator* (Squadron Leader) Alexandru *'Popicu'* Popisteanu, personally led his unit into combat on the 21st. Once the enemy formation had been spotted, he ordered *Cpt av* Alexandru Manoliu, CO of *Esc 57 vân*, to attack the low-flying *Shturmoviks*. Flying with the Rumanians on this day in his own Macchi C.200 was Italian volunteer pilot *Căpitano* Carlo Maurizio Ruspoli, Prince of Poggio Suasa (see *Osprey Aircraft of the Aces 34 - Italian Aces of World War 2*).

While Manoliu (flying 'Yellow 44') led *Escadrila 57 vânătoare* in the attack on the Il-2s, the remaining ten Bf 109E-3s under Popisteanu's command climbed to face the Yaks which were circling above them at 6560 ft. Contrary to Popisteanu's expectations, however, the Soviet fighters did not wait for the Rumanians to make their attack, instead diving at the *Emils* while they were still trying to gain altitude. On the Yak-1s' first high-speed pass, Popisteanu's aircraft was hit in the

Adj maj av Nicolae Burileanu looks in disbelief at the shattered cockpit of his Bf 109E, which was hit by Soviet bullets during a dogfight in 1941. The small calibre projectiles penetrated the cockpit and passed just a few inches from the pilot's head. Despite the damage, Burileanu returned safely to base. He ended the war with at least ten kills, including three air and one ground victories achieved in 1941

A pilot of *Grupul 7 vânătoare* sits in the cockpit of his colourful Bf 109E. The Daimler-Benz engine has just been cranked into life (note the mechanic with the crank handle in his left hand) and the aircraft is ready for a combat sortie over the Odessa area in the autumn of 1941. The eight oblique markings painted beneath the cockpit do not match the known score of any *vânător*, so it is therefore believed that they denote a combination of air and ground victories, as well as 'effective' ground attacks. Although the pilot's identity is uncertain, a former comrade exclaimed when seeing the print that, 'Only Adjutant (Stefan) Greceanu had such a big nose!' *Adj av* Greceanu ended the 1941 campaign with seven victories

Adj stag rez av Stefan Greceanu of Grupul 7 vânătoare poses for the camera in the cockpit of his Bf 109E in late 1941. By the end of the ARR's first campaign he had achieved ace status by downing six Soviet aircraft (one unconfirmed) in 78 combat sorties. By 1945, Adj av Greceanu had been credited with shooting down two more aircraft, as well as having two more unconfirmed, increasing his final tally to 11 victories

fuselage and cockpit. The 37-year-old pilot was wounded, but instead of baling out, he tried to land the stricken fighter near Marienthal. It crashed and he was killed in what was his 33rd combat sortie. Popisteanu's comrades reported six Yaks shot down in the battle, but this could not make up for the loss of their CO. King Michael, who visited the airfield of Gr 7 vân, placed his personal Mihai Vitezul Order on Popisteanu's makeshift coffin as a gesture of appreciation. Later, Grupul 7 vânătoare would include Popisteanu's name in its official designation.

The next day, to boost morale, the CO of Flotila 1 vânătoare, Căpitan comandor aviator (Wing Commander) Mihail Romanescu – known as 'Leul' or 'The Lion' for his strong character – personally took command of Grupul 7 vânătoare.

On 28 August both sides logged a large number of sorties. There were several dogfights, and heroic deeds too. For example, Ml Lt Ivan S Berishvili – a Navy pilot of 8 IAP on loan to 69 IAP – pursued a PZL fighter almost certainly flown by Adj stag av Ion Grama of Gr 3 vân. Close to Karlstadt, the low-flying PZL crashed and Berishvili also hit the ground seconds later. The official Soviet history claims that the Rumanian aircraft was rammed by Berishvili. The Rumanians also claimed another ramming victory by Adj stag rez av Ioan Florea of Esc 44 vân, Gr 3 vân with his P.11F 'White 137' south-west of Vākārjani. Unlike his comrade, Florea survived the incident and returned the next day to tell his story.

The Rumanians also lost an IAR 80 and two P.11Fs on the 28th, while another pair of PZL fighters returned from combat riddled with bullet holes. The Soviets, too, suffered significant losses. Amongst those to fall was ace Leytenant

Photographed in September 1941 on the Odessa front, Adj stag av Ioan Mucenica of Escadrila 56 vânătoare, Grupul 7 vânătoare, enjoys a cigarette whilst perched on the cockpit sill of his Emil, which is parked on the edge of the forest at Salz airfield. Mucenica made a remarkable start to his first campaign, downing seven Soviet aircraft, amounting to eight ARR victories, by October 1941. This score elevated him to 12th place in the unofficial ARR 1941 victory list. By the time he was severely wounded in action on 26 July 1944, Mucenica's tally had reached an impressive 27 victories (from 150 aerial battles), despite his usual assignment as wingman for officer pilots – a role which presented him with fewer chances to claim kills. Confined to hospital for many months, he did not recover in time to add to his 450+ combat sorties

Vitaliy T Topol'skiy, *escadrille* adjutant of 69 IAP. Credited with four individual and four shared victories, he fell in combat with five Rumanian fighters near Krasnyi Pereselenets (in the Freudenthal area). Topol'skiy was posthumously proclaimed Hero of the Soviet Union, but it is not known how he met his death as Rumanian airmen and flak gunners claimed no less than 30 enemy aircraft that day.

The climax in the battle for Odessa came four weeks later when Soviet troops formed a bridgehead at Chebanka-Grigorievka during the night of 21/22 September. Since the Rumanian 4th Army's right flank was seriously endangered by this manoeuvre, GAL headquarters ordered all available aircraft to attack Soviet troops advancing north under strong air cover. On the 22nd, 94 Rumanian aircraft – 62 of them fighters – were sent to the area controlled by the Red Army. In ten hours of combat, nine VVS aircraft were reported shot down in air battles, with a tenth remaining unconfirmed. Despite Soviet claims for over 20 enemy aircraft destroyed, only one Rumanian fighter was actually shot down by the VVS. Another four ARR and one Italian aircraft were either lost to flak or destroyed on the ground.

The Rumanian pilots' effort seriously hindered the Soviet push, which gradually lost momentum and ended in withdrawal during the night of 4/5 October. There were heavy losses on both sides, and the fortress of Odessa finally fell to the Rumanians on 16 October to end their first campaign in the east.

Lt av Ioan Micu, top scoring IAR 80 pilot of the 1941 campaign with 11 victories, points to the damage inflicted on his fighter's fuselage by a Soviet bullet. During the ARR's first campaign, Micu logged an impressive 112 combat sorties, including five strafing missions, and downed eight enemy aircraft in just ten aerial battles. Micu ended the war as a *Căpitan av* with 13 victories

A village school teacher in civilian life, *Adj stag rez av* Tiberiu Vinca was one of the ARR's top fighter aces with at least 17 victories. He is seen here in the cockpit of his *Emil* in the autumn of 1941 during the ARR's first campaign, when he scored at least seven victories. Vinca was mistakenly shot down and killed by the rear gunner of a Luftwaffe He 111 on 12 March 1944

THE RECKONING

Once the tumult of battle had subsided, the results achieved by the ARR's fighter arm in the 1941 campaign could be considered. Between 22 June and 16 October, GAL reported a total of 4739 fighter sorties performed during the course of 858 missions – 329 escort, 193 short-range reconnaissance, 113 airfield protection, 112 interception, 80 free hunting, 24 low level attack and seven surveillance. To these figures could be added two additional dive-bombing missions carried out by ten IAR 81s. A total of 266 enemy aircraft were claimed destroyed in the air or on the ground by all branches of GAL, including the flak batteries, while another 215

remained unconfirmed. Officially, GAL acknowledged the loss of only 16 fighters during the 118 days of action, but the real figure is obviously higher.

The entire fighter force flew a total of 8514 sorties during the campaign. There were 217 aerial battles over Bessarabia, Trans-Dnestra (Transnistria in Rumanian) or Rumania proper. In 4417 hours flown, *Flotila 1 vânătoare* claimed 145 confirmed and 18 unconfirmed enemy aircraft destroyed in the air and 47 on the ground. *Flotila 2 vânătoare* reported 102 aircraft shot down and 24 destroyed on their airfields, while *Flotila 3 vânătoare* was credited with a tally of 57 confirmed kills during the 5575 flying hours logged by its pilots. This amounts to a grand total of 304 aircraft destroyed in the air and 71 on the ground by the *vânători*. Total ARR claims, including those of bomber gunners and flak, reached approximately 600 VVS aircraft.

The majority of these huge claims were obviously fictitious, as the total number of Soviet combat aircraft operating over the southern front was no more than 250 to 300. As not all were destroyed, it seems that the Rumanian pilots and gunners had over-claimed by a factor of three. But they were not alone. Soviet airmen also claimed an unrealistically large number of Axis aircraft destroyed, and it is likely that the VVS over-claimed to an even higher extent.

In terms of confirmed aircraft shot down in combat, the top scoring Rumanian ace of the Bessarabian campaign was *Locotenent de rezervă aviator* Nicolae Polizu of the Bf 109E-equipped *Grupul 7 vânătoare* with eight kills, amounting to nine ARR victories. But Hurricane pilot *Adjutant sef aviator* (flight sergeant) Andrei Rădulescu of *Escadrila 53 vânătoare* achieved seven confirmed and four unconfirmed kills, amounting to at least 14 victories when the unique ARR scoring system was observed. Indeed, applying Rumanian criteria, there were

Photographed upon returning from the ARR's first campaign, several *Grupul 7 vânătoare* pilots relax near hangars at their Pipera base on a warm autumn day in 1941. They are, from left to right, *Adj stag rez av* Tiberiu Vinca (17+ victories), *Slt rez av* Ioan Simionescu (5+), *Adj maj av* Nicolae Burileanu (10+) and *Adj av* Ioan Mucenica (27). The backdrop to this photo is provided by Bf 109E 'Yellow 35' (Wk-Nr. 2480), which features one victory bar forward of the cockpit. This aircraft was often flown by Simionescu

The Hurricane-equipped independent *Escadrila 53 vânătoare* was the most effective ARR fighter squadron of the 1941 campaign. By the time the Bessarabia and Odessa campaign came to an end in mid-October, its pilots had amassed almost 100 victories. The unit lost only a single pilot in return, five-victory ace *Cpt av* Ioan Rosescu being killed on 12 September 1941 in a dogfight with I-16s of the 69th IAP over Gross Liebenthal, near Mayaki. 'Puiu' Rosescu's only successes had been an I-16 bagged on 3 September and two unidentified VVS bombers reportedly destroyed minutes before he was himself shot down. Standing in front of the much-photographed Hurricane 'Yellow 3' are, from left to right (with their respective total scores in 1941 in brackets), *Serg T.R av* Nicolae Culcer (one victory), *Adj av* Anton Sârbu, *Adj stag av* Constantin Popescu (six), unidentified, *Lt av* Horia Agarici (nine), squadron CO *Cpt av* Emil Georgescu (eight), *Adj sef av* Andrei Rădulescu (top scoring ARR ace of 1941 with 14+ victories), *Adj av* Vasile Lagara, unidentified groundcrewman, *Adj stag av* Radu Costache (two) and groundcrewman *Maistru mecanic* Petre. The three top scoring aces of the 1941 campaign were all Hurricane pilots. This photo was taken at Mamaia, on the shores of the Black Sea, which was *Esc 53 vân's* home airfield

46 pilots who became aces, although by Western standards only 18 scored five or more confirmed aerial kills. Despite these successes, the enemy regarded the ARR fighter pilots as less dangerous adversaries than those of the Luftwaffe. A Soviet source states;

'Luckily for pilots of the OdVO (Odessa Military District), the majority of their opponents were Rumanians. They were not found to be as skilled and dangerous as their German colleagues, and could not take advantage of the existing drawbacks of the VVS. The obsolescence of several Rumanian aircraft types – such as the PZL P.11 and P.24, similar to our I-15 – had also been shown.'

By the end of the year, 59 fighters had been lost in combat or in accidents – 20 IAR 80/81s, 18 PZL P.11Fs, nine Bf 109Es, five He 112Bs, three PZL P.24Es, two PZL P.11cs and two Hurricanes. This figure represents 18 per cent, almost one in five, of the total number of fighters available on the first day of war or received at the front as replacements. Human losses were also high. During the four months of combat at least 41 fighter pilots were killed in action or in accidents. But with Odessa harbour captured, the Rumanian airmen could go home for rest, as well as to re-organise and re-equip.

Between 17 October 1941 and 1 August 1942, there was little opportunity for combat for Rumanian fighter pilots. They flew only 1021 sorties – mainly reconnaissance missions. And when they scrambled, it was usually to intercept Soviet reconnaissance aircraft approaching from the Black Sea. As a result, only seven VVS aircraft were claimed destroyed in combat and three on the ground or water.

Back home, following the re-organisation of the fighter arm, most PZL aircraft were withdrawn from frontline duty and the type relegated to training tasks. The majority of squadrons flying Polish fighters received the IAR 80, which was the only aircraft available in sufficient numbers. Apart from 15 second-hand Bf 109E-4s and E-7s, barely enough to replace those lost through attrition, no new fighters were delivered from outside Rumania.

23

TURNING POINT AT STALINGRAD

The Rumanians' major commitment to the Axis war effort in 1942 was made at Stalingrad. The air element of the expeditionary corps was still called *Gruparea Aeriană de Luptă* (GAL), but the main combat component was now concentrated in a separate unit called *Corpul Aerian Român* (Rumanian Air Corps, or CAR). There were two fighter groups attached to CAR, the Bf 109E-equipped *Grupul 7 vânătoare* (*Escadrile 56, 57* and *58*) and *Grupul 8 vânătoare* (*Escadrile 41, 42* and *60*) with the IAR 80A/B. Alongside these two units, the dive-bombing *Grupul 6 bopi* (*Escadrile 61* and *62*) was also sent to the front with IAR 81s, plus a few Bf 109Es. The total number of ARR fighter and fighter/dive-bomber aircraft available in the Stalingrad area in the autumn of 1942, therefore, was just under 100.

GAL headquarters moved to the combat zone in late August, with its combat units following in September. The first fighter group to start operations was *Grupul 8 vânătoare*, followed by *Grupul 6 bopi*. Both were based at Tuzov airfield, some 12.5 miles behind the frontline. Led by *Căpitan aviator* Gheorghe Crihană, *Grupul 7 vânătoare* arrived at the end of September. Its designated base was initially Tuzov, although the unit moved a week later to Karpovka. Bf 109 pilots started combat missions in early October in support of German and Rumanian forces advancing towards the outskirts of Stalingrad.

Between September and November, the main task of the CAR fighter pilots was to escort Luftwaffe and ARR bombers, although airfield protection, free hunt and weather reconnaissance missions were also flown. With the temperature usually well below freezing, and icy winds blowing at up to 60 mph, each take-off was a struggle.

Between 7-10 September the IAR fighters of *Grupul 8 vânătoare* shot down three of the Pe-2 bombers which were making daily attacks on their airfield. Air battles were also frequent in the Stalingrad area, and several MiGs and Yaks were reported shot down by Rumanian fighter pilots. There were losses too, and not only in combat. Even before the first shots had been fired, two IAR 80 pilots had been killed in a mid-air collision. Other airmen and groundcrew subsequently lost their lives in attacks by Soviet fighters and bombers, and several aircraft were destroyed on the ground at Tuzov.

Once in combat, the IAR 81 dive-bomber pilots of *Grupul 6 bopi* proved to be no luckier than their comrades flying the IAR 80. Although there was limited success, they lost several aircraft and pilots either to the enemy or in accidents.

The élite *Grupul 7 vânătoare*, which shared Karpovka airfield with the Luftwaffe, enjoyed more success, as the unit was under virtual German command, receiving supplies from the same source. The Messerschmitt pilots flew four or five sorties every day, weather permitting. Like the IAR 80 units, the group flew mainly escort, reconnaissance and free hunt missions. Air battles were few due to the lack of enemy activity and the foul weather. Nevertheless, a handful of victories were still reported, together with the loss of *Cpt av* Alexandru Manoliu, CO of *Escadrila 57 vânătoare*, on 12 September. He was replaced by *Lt av* Alexandru Serbănescu, who, although new to

Adj sef av Nicolae Burileanu poses alongside his Bf 109E shortly after his arrival on the Stalingrad front on 7 September 1942. His tunic is decorated with the Rumanian pilot's wings, a German *Frontflugspange*, the ribbon of the Iron Cross, Second Class, and an impressive array of miniature decorations. Burileanu was one of the 'old hands' of *Grupul 7 vânătoare*, and by the end of the war the 36-year-old pilot had scored at least ten victories. He subsequently became one of the few *vânători* to succeed in post-war aviation, retiring after 32 years' service, and having flown a total of 50 types of aircraft combat, was destined to become one of the ARR's top-scoring aces.

Despite the loss of Manoliu, and his Bf 109E, together with two IAR 80Bs ('White 16' and 'White 186'), 12 September proved to be a successful day for the *vânători*. They were credited with seven confirmed and five unconfirmed kills, all Yaks. The next day was also fruitful, with four confirmed and five unconfirmed kills for the loss of one IAR 80. The successes continued on 14 September when five Yak-1s were claimed over the River Volga, east of Stalingrad. One IAR 80 was lost in combat, *Adj av* Vasile Teodorescu of *Gr 6 vân* baling out over enemy lines – he was never seen again. It is possible that he was the victim of a *'taran'* (ramming attack) by *Sn Lt* Sergey D Luganskiy of 270 IAP, who claimed a 'Rumanian He 112' by striking it with the wing of

Adj stag rez av Vinca sits in his colourful, refurbished, Bf 109E-7 'Yellow 64' Wk-Nr. 704, which had previously served with *Ergänzungsstaffel* JG 52. Note the personal monogram just visible below the cockpit, the five victory marks and the chalked inscription, indicating the Rumanians' objective at this stage of the war. Vinca flew with *Grupul 7 vânătoare* during the Stalingrad campaign of 1942/43, claiming a confirmed victory over a Soviet Hurricane in the Kudinov area on 20 January 1943

his Yak-1. The next day another three victories were reported, followed by four on the 16th and another five on the 17th. Bad weather then halted further activity.

SOVIET OFFENSIVE

The Red Army's winter offensive began in the sector held by the Rumanian 3rd and 4th Armies on 19 and 20 November 1942, respectively. This shifted the focus of air operations to ground support for troops cut off from the rear and cover for transport aircraft supplying the encircled units. In the days following the Soviet onslaught, *Grupul 7 vânătoare* also found itself cut off. Once the seriousness of the situation was realised, personnel at Karpovka prepared for defence, and the airfield's few flak guns were organised in an artillery role, their primary job being to protect the aircraft. This was done just in time, for at dusk on 22 November, the first Red Army reconnaissance vehicle appeared on the horizon and was quickly knocked out by the flak guns.

Before dawn the next day Soviet tanks arrived in strength. Rumanian deliberations on how to meet this threat were cut short by the tanks firing across the airfield. For the airmen, there was only one solution – take to the air, regardless of the attacks and the darkness. Accordingly, all 16 airworthy Bf 109Es were hastily prepared for a night take-off for which their pilots were not trained. Radio equipment and armour was stripped from each fighter to make room for a passenger – either a pilot whose aircraft was unserviceable or a groundcrewman.

As soon as the aircraft engines were started, the Russian tanks headed for the airfield. The first Messerschmitt attempting to take-off suffered a direct hit and crashed in flames. Then two other fighters collided while taking off in the darkness. Both were set on fire. But the flames helped the other pilots see the makeshift runway and they were able to get airborne. All remaining aircraft were able to escape the hell of Karpovka, as well as the nearby airfields not yet overrun by the Soviets. But the crews of the Rumanian flak guns stayed to fight, and most were killed or captured. Twelve Bf 109Es were left behind to fall into Soviet hands, together with large quantities of ammunition, fuel and other matériel.

The Rumanian retreat continued well into the New Year, with fighter pilots continuing to evacuate one airfield after the other. IAR 80/81-equipped *Grupuri 6* and *8* were finally withdrawn to Rumania in mid-January 1943. By then, their pilots had claimed 26 kills, plus 15 confirmed and two unconfirmed victories, in 33 aerial battles. Some 14 aircraft were in turn lost in combat, together with 11 in accidents and six captured.

Thanks to an infusion of replacement aircraft from German stocks, *Grupul 7 vânătoare* soldiered on alongside the few surviving He 111Hs at Stalino – this *ad hoc* group comprised ten Bf 109Es and six He 111Hs. After limited activity with its few serviceable aircraft, this last ARR unit was ordered back to Rumania in mid-February. By the time of the final withdrawal, Messerschmitt pilots had claimed nine Yak-1s, two Hurricanes and one 'Curtiss' shot down, plus three enemy aircraft destroyed on the ground. *Gr 7 vân* lost 22 Bf 109Es either in combat, in accidents or just abandoned during the retreat.

The top ace of the Stalingrad campaign in respect to overall claims was *Adj av* Teodor Zăbavă of *Grupul 8 vânătoare* with six victories. His score comprised three Yaks confirmed as destroyed in aerial combat, plus another Yak and a MiG unconfirmed and a fifth Yak shared with *Adj av* Marian Dumitrascu. But it was *Cpt av* Emil Droc (a former IAR test pilot who volunteered for service with *Grupul 6 vânătoare*) who had the most confirmed kills – two Yaks and two MiGs, plus an unconfirmed ground victory.

A Bf 109E-3 of *Grupul 7 vânătoare* prepares for take-off from Karpovka West airfield, Stalingrad, in November 1942. 'Yellow 45' (Wk-Nr. 2731) survived the Soviet encirclement in late November, when 12 of the group's *Emils* were abandoned. Note the girl's name *Ileana* painted on the engine cowling. 'Yellow 45' soldiered on with *Gr 5 vân* in the coastal patrol role over the western shores of the Black Sea

NEW EQUIPMENT, NEW TASKS

By spring 1943 it was becoming clear to both ARR and Luftwaffe commanders that Rumanian units were equipped with obsolete aircraft. The appearance of a new generation of Soviet fighters, and the new tasks being planned for the ARR, obliged the Germans to equip their most important eastern European ally with more modern aircraft. The first ARR combat squadron to receive the Bf 109G – known to Rumanian airmen as *G-ul* or *Gheul* – was *Escadrila 43 vânătoare*. This squadron, which had previously operated P.11s, was transferred from *Flotila 3 vânătoare* to strengthen *Grupul 7 vânătoare*. Other less experienced pilots of *Grupul 7* were also trained to fly the Bf 109G, as were the aviators within *Grupul 9*.

At the same time, 20 experienced pilots from *Grupul 7 vânătoare* were temporarily transferred to *Jagdgeschwader 3 'Udet'*, one of the élite Luftwaffe fighter units deployed on the eastern front. The intention was not only to teach the Rumanians how to fly the Bf 109G, but also to give them the opportunity to learn combat tactics from the experienced German pilots during active service. Accordingly, selected Rumanian pilots flew to Dnepropetrovsk-South airfield on 11 March 1943. A few days after taking over brand-new Bf 109G-2 and G-4/*Rüstsatz* 2 and *Rüstsatz* 6 aircraft on loan from the Luftwaffe, the unit took off for Pavlograd – the forward base of III./JG 3. The 20

Slt rez av **Ioan Di Cesare of** *Grupul 7 vânătoare*, **a future knight of the select** *Mihai Viteazul* **Order, sits in the cockpit of his** *Emil* **just weeks before converting to the more potent** *Gustav* **in the spring of 1943. His aircraft displays both his personal monogram and the slogan** *Hai fetito!* **('C'mon lassie!'), as well as five oblique bars representing 'efficient' ground attacks performed in the opening phase of the war with the USSR in 1941 – they do not appear in the pilot's overall score. Di Cesare, born to an Italian father and Rumanian mother, ended the war with at least 23 victories. Today, 87-year-old** *Gen av (r)* **Di Cesare is chairman of one of the two Rumanian veteran airmen's associations, and leader of a minor royalist political party**

In mid-March 1943, selected *Grupul 7 vânătoare* pilots were temporarily transferred to Bf 109G-equipped JG 3 *'Udet'* to enable them to learn combat tactics from experienced German pilots. The 20 Rumanians, together with a similar number of Luftwaffe pilots, formed the experimental fighter group *Deutsch-Königlich Rumänischen Jagdverband*, or German-Royal Rumanian Fighter Unit, under the command of 104-kill *Experte* Leutnant Eberhard von Boremski. The latter is seen in this photo, wearing the *Ritterkreuz* at his neck, flanked by *Cpt av* Dan Scurtu (19+) and *Cpt av* Alexandru Serbănescu (55 victories). Von Boremski survived the war, only to spend many years incarcerated in a Russian prison. A veteran of 630 combat missions, he was killed in an accident in Hamburg in December 1963

Right
Adj stag rez av Iosif Moraru of *Escadrila 56 vânătoare, Grupul 7 vânătoare*, shows off his brand new Bf 109G on loan from the Luftwaffe. 'Gâgă' Moraru ended the war credited with at least 13 victories

Three *Deutsch-Königlich Rumänischen Jagdverband* officer-pilots discuss their next sortie whilst studying a map which shows the area surrounding their base at Kramatorskaya. Photographed in the first days of May 1943, they are, from left to right, *Slt av* Liviu 'Puiu' Muresan (ten victories prior to being killed in action on 10 October 1943), *Lt rez av* Nicolae Polizu (11 victories prior to being killed in action on either 2 or 5 May 1943) and *Slt rez av* Ioan Di Cesare (23+)

Rumanians, together with a similar number of German pilots, formed an experimental fighter group – the *Deutsch-Königlich Rumänischen Jagdverband* (German-Royal Rumanian Fighter Unit), under the command of Luftwaffe *Experte* Leutnant Eberhard von Boremski.

During the unit's first combat mission on 29 March, the Rumanian CO, *Locotenent comandor aviator* Radu Gheorghe – who had logged many hours as an instructor, but had little actual combat experience – was shot down by Soviet fighters. However, in spite of this loss, the Rumanians also achieved their first victory when *Adjutant aviator* Ion Panaite claimed an Il-2. Further missions followed in quick succession, and the victory tally mounted. So too did the casualties, among them *Locotenent de rezervă aviator* Nicolae Polizu-Micsunesti, holder of the *Mihai Viteazul* Order. The top ARR fighter ace of the 1941 campaign, Polizu-Micunesti was shot down on 6 May. That same day Rumanian fighter pilots had achieved six aerial victories, half of them attributed to *Ofiter de echipaj clasa a III-a aviator* (Warrant Officer, 3rd class) Ioan Milu, the future third ranking ARR ace.

On 5 June 1943, a big parade was staged at Kirovograd, attended by King Michael, Marshal Ion Antonescu and high-ranking Luftwaffe officers, to mark the official reactivation of *Corpul 1 Aerian Român* (C1AR) and the dissolution of the German-Rumanian fighter unit, which was regretted by both Luftwaffe and ARR pilots. Between 29 March

and 9 May, the Rumanian 'half-group' had sent 583 aircraft over the combat zone on fighter and fighter-bomber sorties, dropped 32,187 lbs of bombs and downed 28 VVS aircraft at a cost of at least three pilots killed.

With the dissolution of the mixed squadron, the Rumanians were ordered to join their parent unit, *Grupul 7 vânătoare*. Proudly wearing the recently-awarded *Jagdflieger der Udetgeschwader* badge (identifying them as fighter pilots of the *'Udet' Geschwader*), the veteran flyers arrived at Tiraspol on 6 June. There, they were joined by others who had completed the conversion onto the Bf 109G. Shortly afterwards the renewed *Grupul 7 vânătoare* – the ARR's top fighter unit at that time – returned to the front to participate in the ARR's third campaign over the rivers Donets and Mius.

THE THIRD CAMPAIGN

On 12 June 1943, the bulk of *Grupul 7 vânătoare* moved its headquarters to the large Mariupol airfield, where the headquarters of *Flotila 1 vânătoare* had also been established. The principal task for the *vânători* was to escort Rumanian and German aircraft in level and dive-bombing, assault and reconnaissance missions.

C1AR started flying combat sorties over the southern extremity of the eastern front, where ground and air activity was intense. Under these circumstances, the veteran fighter pilots made the best use of the experience they had gained with the *'Udet' Geschwader*, achieving an impressive number of aerial victories with their Bf 109s. The scoring was opened by the newly-promoted *Căpitan aviator* Alexandru Serbănescu, CO of *Escadrila 57 vânătoare*, who claimed a Yak fighter on 24 June. His wingman, *Adjutant aviator* Cristea Chirvăsută – a future top scoring NCO ace with 31 aerial victories – matched his commander's kill when he destroyed a second Yak. However, the newer pilots did not fair so well.

During the first week's combat missions, a Bf 109G-4 *celulă* (pair), comprising squadron commander *Cpt av* Octav Penescu and his wingman *Adj av* Mircea Hlusac, got lost over the endless Russian plain. Reading their compasses the opposite way, they continued east instead of west until their fuel was exhausted and they ended up on a Soviet airfield, where they were taken into captivity. On 26 June, they

On 5 June 1943 a parade was held at Kirovograd to mark the successful conclusion of activities by the joint German-Rumanian fighter unit. Here, two rows of Bf 109G-2/G-4s, together with several Fieseler Fi 156 *Storch* liaison aircraft, are lined up for inspection. While the *Gustavs* in the front row appear to be painted in a three-tone grey camouflage scheme (RLM 74/75/76), the uppersurfaces and fuselage of the Bf 109G at left has been over-painted with dark green (RLM 71). Curiously, the aircraft in the front row display double white fuselage identification numbers, one in front and the other aft of the national marking were joined as PoWs by *Adj av* Laurentiu Catanā, who collided with a Soviet Spitfire – which represented his tenth, and final, aerial victory – during the confusion of a dogfight. He baled out over hostile territory. These pilots eventually returned to Rumania long after the war had ended.

Gr 7 vân flew nine missions comprising 48 sorties on 18 July. Eight combat engagements were fought with the VVS in the Kuybishev-Uspenskaya-Slavyyansk area, and by the end of the day the

Cpt av Serbănescu (right), CO of *Escadrila 57 vânătoare* of *Grupul 7 vânătoare*, uses typical fighter pilot gestures to tell his squadronmates about the part he played in a recent aerial engagement. The men watching him are, from right to left, *Lt av* Teodor Greceanu (24+ victories), *Adj av* Gheorghe Firu (one victory prior to being killed in action on 26 August 1943), unidentified (hidden) and *Slt av* Nicolae 'Colea' Naghirneac (six). This photo was taken on the eastern front, probably at Mariupol, in June 1943

Rumanians had claimed a record 20 enemy aircraft destroyed. ARR headquarters later confirmed 15 kills, listing the rest as probables. Two of the confirmed victories were achieved by *Cpt av* Alexandru Serbănescu, along with a third claim unconfirmed, while his rival *Cpt rez av* Constantin Cantacuzino got only one of three claims confirmed.

This single-day record was surpassed only twice on the Soviet front, firstly on 28 August 1941 and then on 16 August 1943. On the latter date, Rumanian fighter pilots were credited with 22 confirmed and five probable kills for the loss of three pilots – the most successful day ever for the *vânători*. These victories, involving Il-2s, LaGGs, Yaks, Airacobras and Bostons, were achieved over Izyum, Kramatorskaya, Dolina Golaya and Bogoroditnoye. That day's top scoring Rumanian pilot was Ioan Milu, who was credited with three Il-2s and two 'B-8' Bostons, equivalent to seven victories under the ARR scoring system, which represented a record for one day.

Returning to July 1943, an interesting detail emerges from the report submitted by Constantin Cantacuzino, who claimed a Yak fighter while escorting a Luftwaffe reconnaissance aircraft on the afternoon of the 27th. Due to the Yak's bright red engine cowling and

Slt rez av Ioan Di Cesare of *Grupul 7 vânătoare* shows engineer *Lt mec* Serban Diaconu the damage to his Messerschmitt ('White 38' Wk-Nr. 13845) after a dogfight with Soviet fighters which were obviously armed with both machine guns and cannon. 'White 38' later suffered 30 per cent damage from Soviet flak while being flown by *Adj av* Constantin Ursache on 21 July 1943, the fighter in turn being handed back to the Germans for repairs to be effected

Grupul 6 vânâtoare pilots enjoy a meal between flights under a hot mid-summer sun at Pipera airfield, near Bucharest, on 13 August 1943. They are, from left to right, unidentified, Lt av Gheorghe Posteucã (two victories), Adj av Gheorghe Cocebas (eight), Lt av Dumitru Baciu (ten official and three unofficial) and Slt av Teodor Nicolaescu (two). Parked behind them is 'White 301', which was the initial aircraft of the final IAR 81C series production batch. Note that the fighter has been fitted with an unusually long non-standard spinner. 'White 301' was shot down in a dogfight with USAAF fighters on 18 May 1944

its pilot's flying skills, Cantacuzino presumed his victim to be an ace. Soviet sources state that only one of their top pilots was lost in aerial combat that day – Sn Lt Nikolay F Khimushin of 106 GIAP, 11 GIAD, 1 GSAK, 17 VA, who was killed in action over Kupyansk in his Yak-1. By the time of his death, he had flown 192 missions, taken part in 49 combats and claimed 11 kills. Khimushin was posthumously awarded the title of 'Hero of the Soviet Union'.

On 14 August 1943, nine pilots of Grupul 9 vânâtoare who had completed the transition course from the IAR 80 to the Bf 109G at Tiraspol were ordered to Kramatorskaya to join Grupul 7 vânâtoare. Victories accumulated rapidly, and the old hands who wore the 'Udet' badge on their tunics added significantly to their scores. But sometimes skill, experience and courage were not enough to overcome the enemy's overwhelming numerical superiority. On 17 August no fewer than six Rumanian Bf 109Gs were hit in combat. Among them was 'White 28' (Wk-Nr. 19528), piloted by Slt av Costin Georgescu of Escadrila 43 vânâtoare, who was seriously injured in a dogfight with 15 Yaks and ended up in hospital, where his left arm was amputated.

In early September, Kramatorskaya airfield was threatened by rapidly-advancing Soviet tanks and had to be evacuated. Serviceable

This Bf 109G-4 (Wk-Nr. 19522) was the 31st of 44 Gustavs lent by the Luftwaffe to the Rumanians for frontline use only in March 1943. Flown by Of ech av Ioan Milu of Grupul 7 vânâtoare, it sustained 35 per cent damage in combat with a LaGG-3 flown by a VVS ace on 19 August 1943. The fighter was returned to the Germans for repair and replaced with another Gustav, numbered 'White 31A' by the ARR

'White 24' was belly-landed by *Adj stag rez av* Iosif 'Joshka' Moraru (13 victories) of *Grupul 7 vânătoare* near Kramatorskaya airfield on 18 August 1943, although German documents indicate that this incident occurred the day before. The accident was caused by pilot error, and the aircraft (Wk-Nr. 19607) suffered 30 per cent damage, resulting in it being handed back to the Germans for repair. 'White 24' was replaced by G-2 Wk-Nr. 13902, and coded 'White 24A'. Note how the original Luftwaffe *Balkenkreuze* on the wings and fuselage have been over-painted with light grey and the Rumanian markings applied on top. The *Hakenkreuz* on the fin and the Luftwaffe unit emblem below the cockpit have been over-painted with the same colour

fighters were sent to Dnepropetrovsk and Mariupol, while damaged ones went to Melitopol. Later in the month *Grupul 7 vânătoare* moved to Genichesk, where it received the first Bf 109G-6s.

The Rumanians suffered more losses on 10 October when all the *Gustavs* in a four-ship *patrulă* were shot down in a dogfight with Airacobras over Molotnoye Liman on the northern shores of the Azov Sea. This was a uniquely grim record for the *vânători* in its clashes with the Soviets. One Rumanian, *Slt av* Liviu Muresan, a ten-victory ace flying Bf 109G-4 'White 36b' (Wk-Nr. 19806), was killed. The sole victory claimed was that by *Adj stag av* Constantin Nicoară, who was himself wounded in combat. One of the pilots shot down was *Cpt av* Serbănescu, then top-scoring ARR ace. He crash-landed his burning Bf 109G-6 'White 44' (Wk-Nr. 15854) close to the frontline and was rescued by Rumanian mountain troops.

The legendary 9 GvIAD (the main unit of some of the most famous VVS aces, including Pokryshkin, Klubov, Golubev and Glinka) was operating in that area from Rozovka airfield, although no matching claims have yet been identified. Soviet propaganda immediately stated that with the destruction of four Bf 109Gs and the loss of the group CO, the elite *Gr 7 vân* was virtually annihilated. A Rumanian pilot reportedly responded to this radio announcement by flying over the

Of ech cl III av Ioan Maga, one of the top ARR aces, adjusts his throat microphone with the help of a groundcrewman prior to flying a sortie in July 1944. Not only is Maga's aircraft of German manufacture, but also his clothing and equipment. By the end of the war, the ace had flown approximately 200 combat sorties, participated in over 50 aerial battles and achieved a total of 29 victories. He was seventh in the unofficial Rumanian ace listing

nearest VVS airfield and dropping a note inviting a VVS delegation to visit the Rumanian base under a flag of truce to meet Serbănescu in person. The Soviets did not take up the offer, however – the days of aerial chivalry were apparently long past.

In late October, more freshly-trained pilots of *Grupul 9 vânătoare* (*Escadrile 47, 48* and *56*) arrived from Tiraspol to replace their exhausted *Grupul 7 vânătoare* comrades. Several experienced pilots from *Grupul 7* stayed with them, however, while the others returned home for a rest after five months of continuous frontline duty.

A gathering of aces. These five leading ARR fighter pilots assembled at Mariupol, in the Ukraine, on 30 August 1943 in order to receive Rumania's highest wartime decoration for officers, the *Mihai Viteazul* Order, Third Class. They are, from left to right, *Cpt av* Constantin Cantacuzino, *Slt rez av* Ioan Di Cesare, *Lt av* Teodor Greceanu, *Cpt av* Alexandru Serbănescu and *Of ech cl III av* Ioan Milu. When this official photograph was taken, these five airmen had shot down over 85 Soviet aircraft between them, and by the end of the war this total (both confirmed and probable) had exceeded 187, most of which were downed in aerial combat while flying the highly regarded Bf 109. This represented a total of 223 victories according to the ARR scoring system, which was an astonishing feat for pilots serving with a small Axis air force. Only Serbănescu failed to survive the war

FACING THE *TIDAL WAVE*

While *Grupul 7 vânătoare* fought superior numbers of VVS aircraft over the USSR, the home front remained inactive. Rumanian day fighter pilots continued conversion training on German aircraft at the Luftwaffe-run fighter schools at Galati and Tiraspol.

It seemed quiet on the morning of Sunday, 1 August 1943, and all over Rumania military personnel and civilians were enjoying the warm summer day. So too were the few pilots and other ARR personnel still on their airfields, for the Rumanians were unaware of a new threat heading towards them from the south-west. Unexpectedly, at 1300 hrs, a huge loose formation of pink-painted four-engined bombers penetrated Rumanian airspace, breaking the stillness of the early afternoon. Once close to their target, which turned out to be the Ploiesti oilfields, the bombers dropped to tree-top level, but did not remain undetected. The chain of German *Freya* radar stations in Wallachia (southern Rumania) picked up strong signals just in time to warn German and Rumanian fighters and flak defences of the threat.

When the air raid warning sirens sounded, both German and Rumanian flyers assumed it was just another drill. Nevertheless, they scrambled and headed towards the zone indicated by *Tigrul* ('Tiger', which was the code name of the fighter control centre at Pipera, near Bucharest). The defenders were seeking the enemy at high altitude, but they spotted a huge formation of large bombers flying at a mere 500 ft above the oil refineries and storage tanks. Once the enemy formation was detected at 1400 hrs, German and Rumanian fighters dived on it at high speed. Shouts, commands and curses in English, German and Rumanian filled the airwaves. The ensuing battle raged for less than an hour, but it was equally fierce and bloody for both sides. The Americans suffered heavily – out of about 130 B-24 Liberators which reached the target, at least 36 fell to fighters and flak.

Once the noise of battle had subsided, the defenders could count their victories and losses. According to Rumanian statistics, ARR

Co-operation between Luftwaffe fighter units and the ARR's IAR 80/81-equipped squadrons was rare, and when they did get together, it was mainly for propaganda purposes. A fictitious joint exercise involving German pilots is depicted here, and amongst the men being briefed is Hauptmann Wilhelm 'Willi' Steinmann, *Staffelkapitän* of 1./JG 4. The Rumanian pilots, wearing field caps, are all from *Escadrila 53 vânătoare* – *Lt av* Horia Pop (two victories), *Lt av* Ion Galea (12) and *Adj av* Valeriu 'Bimbo' Buzdugan (no score), the latter sitting on the IAR 80's port wing. Note the unit's mounted 'Mickey Mouse' emblem applied to the IAR 80A in the background. Curiously, the latter lacks the usual blue-yellow-red vertical stripes on its replacement rudder

As previously mentioned, co-operation between ARR and Luftwaffe units was infrequent, although Rumanian and German Bf 109Gs sometimes made joint attacks against USAAF formations in missions called *Sternflug* (literally 'Star Flight'). However, close collaboration among units equipped with different aircraft types was virtually non-existent. Therefore, this photograph of a Luftwaffe Bf 109G – believed to be from III./JG 4 – sandwiched between two IAR 81Cs was probably posed for propaganda purposes only

fighters – Bf 109Gs of *Escadrila 53 vânătoare*, attached to the mixed German-Rumanian I./JG 4 (called *Ölschutzstaffel Ploesti* or Oil Protection Unit Ploesti), IAR 80/81s of *Escadrile 61* and *62* of *Grupul 6 vânătoare* and *Escadrila 45* of *Grupul 4 vânătoare*, as well as Bf 110Cs of *Escadrila 51 vânătoare de noapte* (the ARR's only nightfighter squadron) – were confirmed as having shot down ten

B-24Ds, with two probables. They had lost an IAR 80B and a Bf 110C, one airman being killed and two others wounded. Several other fighters force landed due to combat damage or fuel shortage.

The Luftwaffe reported seven B-24Ds destroyed for the loss of a Bf 109G and a Bf 110E and two airmen killed. The effective anti-aircraft defences were eventually credited with 17 bombers from the 35 initially claimed. It lost 15 personnel. Undoubtedly, more Liberators had been severely damaged over Rumania to crash or force-land en-route to their North African bases.

USAAF commanders and the American media declared Operation *Tidal Wave* a success. If so, it was a pyrrhic victory. The Ploiesti oil refineries were not knocked out as intended, only damaged, and production returned to pre-attack levels within weeks. The price paid by the Americans for this limited result was enormous, however. Another unwanted effect of this daring raid, not felt by the USAAF until the following year, was the re-organisation and reinforcement of the joint Rumanian-German air defence.

In early April 1944, when the next Allied aircraft penetrated Rumanian airspace, a well-organised and efficient fighter and anti-aircraft defence was encountered. The attackers were virtually decimated, the USAAF and RAF enduring one of the highest loss rates suffered in the whole European theatre of operations.

1944 – YEAR OF THE CRUCIBLE

New Year's Eve 1944 found Rumanian fighter pilots operating on two separate fronts, with a small force fighting on the eastern front and the rest based in the homeland in anticipation of further US bombing raids.

In the east, the main ARR fighter element deployed was *Grupul 9 vânătoare*. On 10 January, in accordance with the shifting of the

This unique shot features the return of an unidentified IAR 81C pilot after he had apparently downed his unit's (possibly *Grupul 4 vânătoare*) 100th enemy aircraft. According to the other sign, it was also the group's 3000th combat sortie, and the two numbers equate to one kill for every 30 combat sorties – a rather poor return for a fighter unit. These details place the event in the winter of 1943/44, when one squadron was always based on the snow-covered north-western shores of the Black Sea, in the Ukraine. Such German-style celebrations with commemorative signs were uncommon in the ARR

Soviet pressure on Rumania caused *Grupul 9 vânătoare* to retreat to Tãtarka airfield near Odessa, in the Trans-Dnestra Region. This photograph of Bf 109G-4 'White 3a' of *Grupul 9 vânătoare* was taken on 12 March 1944 – the very day that the group arrived at its new base. The aircraft's pilot, seen walking towards the camera second from right in Luftwaffe black winter boots, is *Adj stag rez av* Tiberiu Vinca, one of the *Grup's* leading aces with at least 17 victories to his credit. Later that same day, whilst flying his 248th combat sortie, Vinca was killed in error by the rear gunner of a German He 111 as he closed in to identify it

Ten leather-clad IAR 80 pilots of *Escadrila 59 vânătoare, Grupul 6 vânătoare*, line up for an official unit photograph at Popesti-Leordeni airfield on 14 January 1944. They are, from left to right, *Lt av* Dumitru 'Take' Baciu (ten official and three unofficial victories), *Adj av* Aurelian Barbici (three), *Slt av* Constantin Tulică (no score), *Lt av* Eugen Ianculescu (four), two unidentified airmen, *Slt av* Alexandru 'Putzifer' Ionescu (no score), unidentified pilot, *Adj av* Ioan Dimache (ten) and *Cpt av* Petre Constantinescu (five)

frontline, the *Grup* was ordered from Nikolayev back to Lepetika airfield. Then, in early March, it was recalled to Dalnik, near Odessa. Throughout this period, a combination of hostile weather, a lack of proper repair facilities and insufficient spare parts and supplies reduced the fighting abilities of the *Grup* to the strength of only a squadron. For example, on 2 March, *Grupul 9 vânătoare* reported having only 12 serviceable Bf 109Gs.

On 10 April, Soviet advance guards reached the outskirts of Odessa, while Tiraspol, capital of the Trans-Dnestra region under Rumanian administration, fell two days later. Just prior to this, *Grupul 9 vânătoare* had retreated into Rumania proper when it flew to Tecuci airfield, in Moldavia. From here, in concordance with other ARR combat units, it was supposed to stop the Soviet 'steamroller' penetrating into north-eastern Rumania.

In the ensuing aerial battles, which peaked in May, both sides claimed an impressive number of victories. That month alone, ARR fighter pilots received credit for 50 Soviet aeroplanes downed, while another dozen claims remained unconfirmed. By rigorously comparing loss data of both the VVS and ARR with victory claims, one can draw the conclusion that overclaiming was again widespread on both sides. Indeed, in a private letter, a noted Russian aviation researcher approximates that during the May offensive alone, Soviet airmen fighting on the Moldavian front filed four times more claims than actual Axis losses, while he approximates that the Axis side overclaimed three times as many kills – a remarkable, albeit unofficial, admission.

Once back on home soil, Rumanian fighter pilots became more determined to defend their borders not only against the 'Bolshevik menace', but also the 'American sky terrorists', as the USAAF airmen were labelled following their first large-scale attack of 1944. Sent to bomb the main Bucharest *Gara de Nord* railway station and marshalling yard on 4 April, a large number of the attacking B-24Hs from the Fifteenth Air Force missed their target and hit a nearby

37

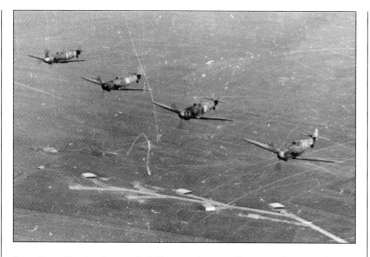

A Bf 109G-2 patrol (equivalent to a Luftwaffe *Schwarm*) of *Escadrila 53 vânātoare, Grupul 7 vânātoare* – comprising aircraft 'White 1', '13', '10' and '3' – lines up in typical *Jagdwaffe*-inspired fighting formation as it overflies its home base in March 1944. The leading aircraft was the white-ruddered 'White 1' at right, which was the usual mount of unit CO, *Cpt av* Lucian Toma, an ace with 13 victories. The sight of such a potent formation would have probably caused great concern for any enemy pilot. Note the white *Spiralschnauze* painted on the spinners (except for 'White 10') and the lack of ARR blue-yellow-red vertical stripes on the rudders

housing district instead, killing 2673 civilians and wounding a further 2341.

ARR and Luftwaffe fighters clashed with the unescorted bombers above Bucharest, downing 11 – the Fifteenth Air Force lists only eight B-24Hs lost over Rumania, one over the Mediterranean and another one over Italy. Pilots of the three IAR 80/81-equipped *Grupuri* (Nos 1, 2 and 6) were initially credited with 28 confirmed aerial victories and 12 probables, and they in turn lost only three aircraft of the 57 that had scrambled, with three pilots being killed in action and three more wounded. Additionally, *Gr 5* and *7 vân* were credited with four and one bombers destroyed respectively, as well as four unconfirmed.

The next day, the *vânātori* received credit for 15 enemy aircraft destroyed – nine B-24Hs and two B-17F/Gs were actually lost over Rumania, along with a P-38F reported missing over Yugoslavia. IAR 80/81 pilots of *Grupul 6 vânātoare* initially claimed 14 aircraft and two probables, without loss, while the identically equipped *Grupul 1 vânātoare* reported three enemy aeroplanes destroyed and two damaged for the loss of two of its own machines. *Grupuri 5* and *7 vânātoare* also engaged the USAAF on this (text continues on page 47)

Seven fighter pilots and two dogs pose for the camera beside Bf 109G-2 'White 1' of *Escadrila 53 vânātoare, Grupul 7 vânātoare*, parked on the concrete runway at Mizil in February 1944. They are, from left to right (standing), *Adj rez av* Casian Teodorescu (three victories), *Slt rez av* Brezeanu (no score), *Lt av* Flaviu Zamfirescu (four victories prior to being killed in action by USAAF fighters on 22 May 1944 while escaping by parachute), *Adj stag av* Dumitru Encioiu (five), *Of ech cl III av* Ioan Maga (29) and *Adj stag rez av* Tiberiu Vinca (17+ victories prior to being killed in error on 12 March 1944). *Adj stag av* Alexandru Economu (five victories prior to being killed in action on 26 July 1944) is kneeling in the foreground playing with the small dog. Vinca wears the German pilot's badge, three rows of miniature decoration bars, the *Frontflugspange* (Front Flight Clasp), the Iron Cross, First Class and the ribbon for the Second Class. The two coloured strings around his left shoulder represent the Orders of *Mihai Viteazul* and the *Virtutea Aeronautiā*, which were awarded to his parent unit. On his left sleeve, above the Rumanian pilot's cloth patch, are two white triangles, which indicate combat wounds. The black band on his left lapel is a sign of mourning. Curiously, he does not wear the Rumanian pilot's badge

COLOUR PLATES

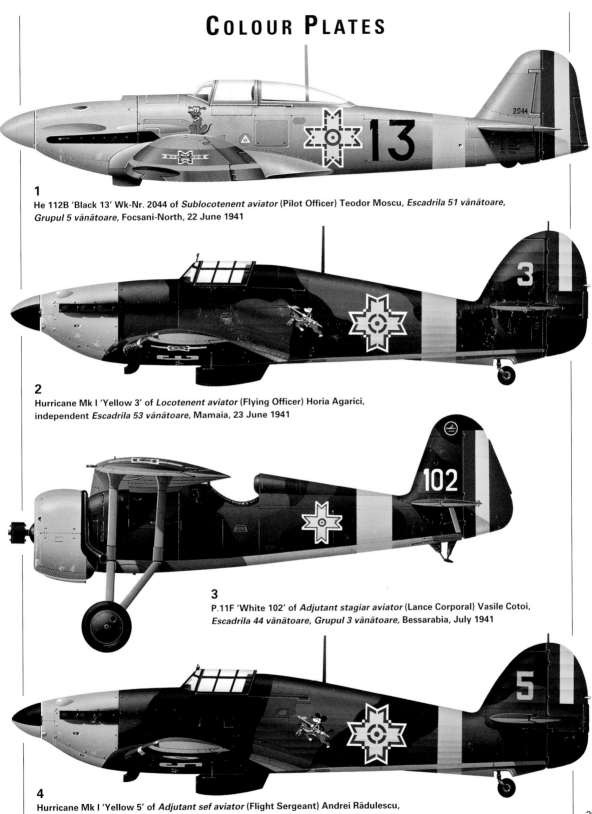

1
He 112B 'Black 13' Wk-Nr. 2044 of *Sublocotenent aviator* (Pilot Officer) Teodor Moscu, *Escadrila 51 vânătoare*, *Grupul 5 vânătoare*, Focsani-North, 22 June 1941

2
Hurricane Mk I 'Yellow 3' of *Locotenent aviator* (Flying Officer) Horia Agarici, independent *Escadrila 53 vânătoare*, Mamaia, 23 June 1941

3
P.11F 'White 102' of *Adjutant stagiar aviator* (Lance Corporal) Vasile Cotoi, *Escadrila 44 vânătoare*, *Grupul 3 vânătoare*, Bessarabia, July 1941

4
Hurricane Mk I 'Yellow 5' of *Adjutant sef aviator* (Flight Sergeant) Andrei Rădulescu, *Escadrila 53 vânătoare*, Salz, July 1941

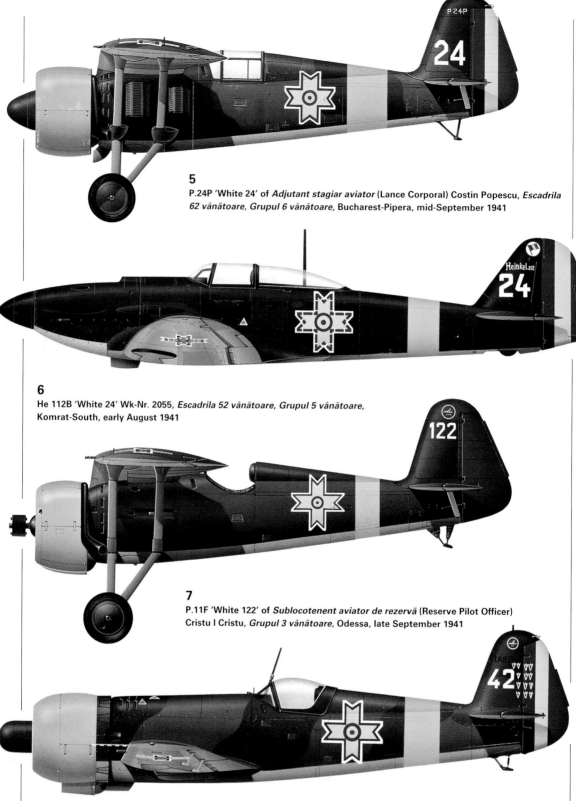

5
P.24P 'White 24' of *Adjutant stagiar aviator* (Lance Corporal) Costin Popescu, *Escadrila 62 vânătoare, Grupul 6 vânătoare*, Bucharest-Pipera, mid-September 1941

6
He 112B 'White 24' Wk-Nr. 2055, *Escadrila 52 vânătoare, Grupul 5 vânătoare*, Komrat-South, early August 1941

7
P.11F 'White 122' of *Sublocotenent aviator de rezervă* (Reserve Pilot Officer) Cristu I Cristu, *Grupul 3 vânătoare*, Odessa, late September 1941

8
IAR 80 'White 42' of *Grupul 8 vânătoare*, Bessarabia, August 1941

9
Bf 109E-3 'Yellow 35' Wk-Nr. 2480 of *Grupul 7 vânătoare, Escadrila 58 vânătoare*, Kishinev (Chisinău), late July 1941

10
IAR 80A 'White 86' of *Locotenent aviator* (Flying Officer) Ioan Micu, *Escadrila 41 vânătoare, Grupul 8 vânătoare*, southern Bessarabia, July 1941

11
Bf 109E-3 'Yellow 26' of *Adjutant stagiar de rezervă aviator* (Reserve Lance Corporal) Stefan Greceanu, *Grupul 7 vânătoare, Escadrila 57 vânătoare*, Salz, Bessarabia, early September 1941

12
Bf 109E-3 'Yellow 11' Wk-Nr. 2729 of *Locotenent aviator* Alexandru Serbănescu, *Grupul 7 vânătoare*, Bucharest-Pipera, late summer 1942

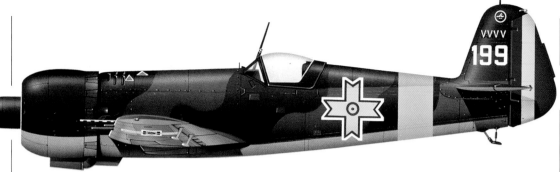

13
IAR 80B 'White 199', of *Căpitan aviator* (Flight Lieutenant) Emil Frideric Droc, CO of *Escadrila 60 vânătoare,*
Grupul 8 vânătoare, Stalingrad area, September 1942

14
Bf 109E-7 'Yellow 64' Wk-Nr. 704 of *Adjutant aviator de rezervă* Tiberiu Vinca, *Grupul 7 vânătoare,*
Stalingrad, late 1942

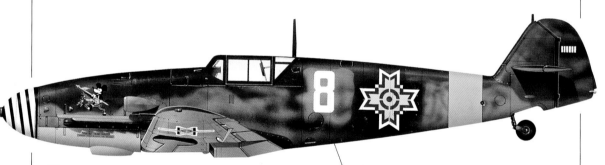

15
Bf 109G-2 'White 8' (believed to be Wk-Nr. 10360) of *Adjutant aviator de rezervă* Stefan 'Bebe' Greceanu,
Escadrila 53 vânătoare, Mizil, July 1943

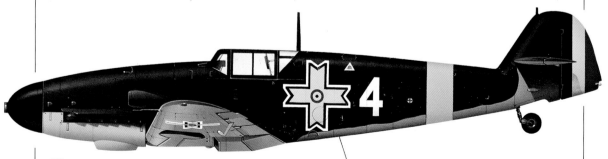

16
Bf 109G-4 'White 4' Wk-Nr. 19546, of *Căpitan de rezervă aviator* (Reserve Flight Lieutenant) Constantin Cantacuzino,
CO of *Escadrila 58 vânătoare, Grupul 7 vânătoare,* southern Ukraine, summer 1943

17
IAR 80C 'White 279' of *Locotenent aviator* (Flying Officer) Ion Bârlădeanu, CO of *Escadrila 45 vânătoare*,
Grupul 4 vânătoare, Târgsorul Nou airfield, near Ploiesti, August 1943

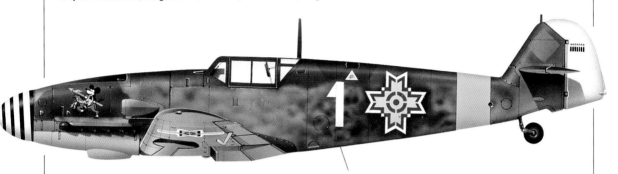

18
Bf 109G-2 'White 1' (believed to be Wk-Nr. 14680) of *Escadrila 53 vânătoare*,
attached to the joint German-Rumanian I./JG 4, Mizil, August 1943

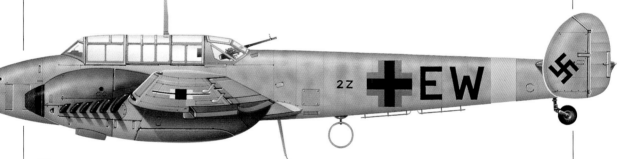

19
Bf 110C-1 'Black 2Z+EW' Wk-Nr. 1819, of 12./NJG 6 (Luftwaffe unit designation), referred to in Rumanian documents as
Escadrila 51 vânătoare de noapte, Ploiesti, 1 August 1943

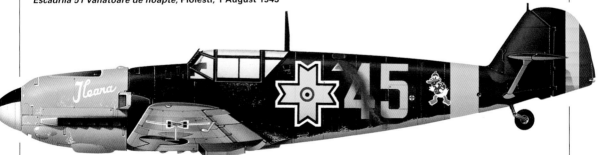

20
Bf 109E-3 'Yellow 45' Wk-Nr. 2731 of *Căpitan aviator* Gheorghe Iliescu, CO of *Grupul 5 vânătoare*, *Escadrila 52 vânătoare*,
Mamaia, summer 1943

21
Hs 129B-2 'White 126a' Wk-Nr. 141274 of *Adjutant aviator* (Corporal) Teodor Zăbavă,
Grupul 8 asalt (8th Assault Group), October 1943

22
Bf 109E-4 'Yellow 47' Wk-Nr. 2643 of *Sublocotenent aviator* (Pilot Officer) Ion Galea,
Grupul 5 vânătoare, Escadrila 52 vânătoare, Mamaia, late 1943

23
IAR 81C 'White 341' of *Sublocotenent aviator* (Pilot Officer) Dumitru 'Take' Baciu,
Grupul 6 vânătoare, Popesti-Leordeni, February 1944

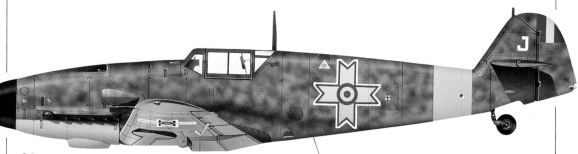

24
Bf 109G-4 'White J' of *Căpitan aviator* (Flight Lieutenant) Dan Scurtu, *Escadrila 57 vânătoare*,
Grupul 7 vânătoare, Leipzig, Bessarabia, late April 1944

25
IAR 80A 'White 97' of *Adjutant aviator* (Corporal) Dumitru Chera,
Grupul 1 vânătoare, Ploiesti, 5 May 1944

26
IAR 81C 'White 344' of *Căpitan aviator* (Flight Lieutenant) Dan-Valentin Vizanty,
CO of *Grupul 6 vânătoare*, Popesti-Leordeni airfield, 10 June 1944

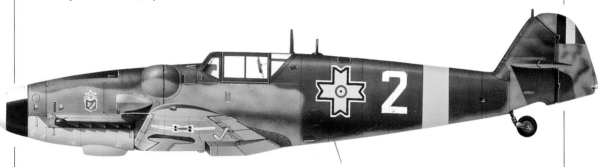

27
Bf 109G-6 'White 2' (possibly Wk-Nr. 166161) of *Escadrila 47 vânătoare, Grupul 9 vânătoare*, July 1944

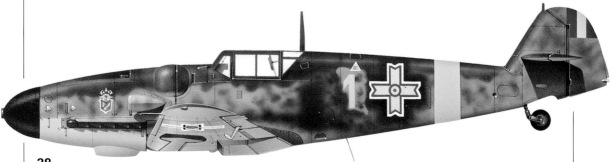

28
Bf 109G-6 'Yellow 1' of *Căpitan aviator* Alexandru Serbănescu, CO *Grupul 9 vânătoare*, August 1944

29
IAR 81C 'White 343' of *Adjutant sef aviator* (Flight Sergeant) Vasile Mirilă,
Grupul 2 vânătoare, 14 September 1944

30
Bf 109G-6 'Yellow 3' Wk-Nr. 165560 of *Locotenent aviator* (Flying Officer) Tudor Greceanu,
Grupul 9 vânătoare, late 1944

31
IAR 81C 'White 319' of *Adjutant aviator* (Corporal) Gheorghe Grecu, *Escadrila 66 vânătoare*,
Grupul 2 vânătoare, Debrecen, Hungary, 9 February 1945

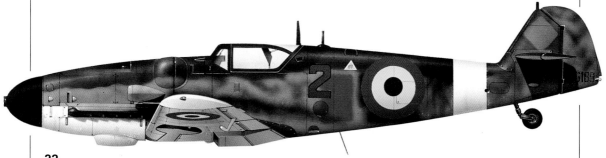

32
Bf 109G-6 'Red 2' Wk-Nr. 166169 of *Grupul 9 vânătoare*, Lucenec (Losonc), February 1945

day, its pilots claiming four and three Liberators destroyed, respectively.

On 21 April, IAR 80/81 pilots encountered the long-range P-51B/C Mustangs of the 31st FG for the first time, the American fighters making their debut over Rumania on this date. The defenders were taken completely by surprise, and suffered terrible losses. *Gr 1 vân* had six aircraft shot down, with five pilots being killed and two wounded. *Gr 2 vân* lost four fighters, and two of its pilots were killed and four wounded. Finally, *Gr 6 vân* had four aircraft destroyed and four pilots killed. The ARR did inflict some casualties on the USAAF, however, its pilots being credited with the destruction of six Liberators.

It now became apparent to the ARR HQ that USAAF bombing and strafing missions were here to stay. In order to match this new threat, the High Command boosted its modest home defences with the allocation of the following assets to the anti-bomber mission – Bf 109Es of *Grupul 5 vânātoare* (*Escadrile 51* and *52*), Bf 109Gs of the experienced *Grupul 7 vânātoare* (*Escadrile 53, 57* and *58*), IAR 80/81s of *Grupul 6 vânātoare* (*Escadrile 59, 61* and *62*) and *Grupul 1 vânātoare* (*Escadrila 43*, equipped with Bf 109Gs, and *Escadrile 63* and *64* with the IAR 81). Later, *Grupul 2 vânātoare* (*Escadrile 65, 66* and *67*) was also tasked with home defence, and occasionally *Grupul 3 vânātoare* (*Escadrile 44* and *50*), based at Brasov, also offered its support.

The combined strength of these units usually amounted to no more than 30 Bf 109E/Gs and 70 IAR 80/81s. Some 60 to 80 Luftwaffe Bf 109Gs, plus a few Fw 190s and Bf 110s, could also be counted on. Typically, unserviceability further reduced this force by half. Thus, the large formations of Allied fighters and bombers sent to attack targets in Rumania were opposed by 100-120 Axis fighters at the most, but frequently by a far smaller force.

By mid-April, the Soviet threat at Rumania's north-eastern borders had grown significantly, resulting in *Grupul 7 vânātoare* being transferred on the 20th from Bucharest-Pipera to southern Moldavia to supplement the overwhelmed *Grupul 9 vânātoare*. That same day it participated in morning and afternoon patrols against Soviet forces. In between these missions, the unit manned the standby alert between 1000 and 1400 hrs, when USAAF bomber formations were expected to appear.

Grupul 7's place at Bucharest-Pipera was taken by the largely inexperienced *Grupul 2 vânātoare*, which had been re-formed only three months earlier with IAR 80/81s. Thus, between late April and early May, the ARR's only contribution to the defence of the Rumanian capital were the two IAR 80/81-equipped *Grupuri*. Yet

Brothers-in-arms. Despite the allegations of post-war Rumanian Communist propaganda, Luftwaffe and ARR airmen maintained a close and friendly working relationship throughout their common fight on the eastern front until the Rumanians changed sides on 23 August 1944. Here, the top ARR ace in the fight against the Allies, *Cpt av* Alexandru Serbănescu, links arms with Luftwaffe fighter pilot Leutnant Ludwig Neuböck of JG 52. From February 1944, Neuböck and Unteroffizier Ernst Stengl were posted to *Grupul 9 vânātoare* as liaison pilots. While flying in combat with the Rumanians, Neuböck downed at least two Soviet aircraft from his final total of 32 kills, while Stengl accounted for 11. The other ARR pilots seen here are, from left to right, *Lt av* Teodor Greceanu, *Lt rez av* Ioan Simionescu, *Lt av* Hariton Dusescu and *Lt Av* Mircea Senchea

despite operating an obsolescent fighter, these units battled well against a technically and numerically superior enemy.

For example, according to official Rumanian statistics, between 4 April and 6 June 1944, *Grupul 6 vânătoare* clashed with USAAF aircraft 12 times. A total of 363 IAR 80/81 sorties were flown during this period, and pilots claimed 60 definite and ten probable victories – the unique ARR scoring system means that some 30-40 aircraft could have been shot down. In return, only seven pilots were killed in action.

One of those to die was *Cpt av* Gheorghe Stănică, CO of *Esc 66 vân*, *Gr 2 vân*, who had been credited with 15 aerial victories by the time of his death in combat on 18 May. That same date saw fellow *Esc 66 vân*, *Gr 2 vân*, ace *Slt av* Gheorghe Cristea killed soon after he had claimed his 12th victory. Another eminent pilot to be lost in May was *Adj av* Florian Budu of *Gr 1 vân*, who was one of the leading IAR 80/81 aces with seven aircraft destroyed (equivalent to nine victories) when he was shot down on the 31st. Two other top scoring IAR pilots also fell to their deaths on this day, namely *Lt av* Ioan Bârlădeanu (12 victories) and *Slt av* Petre Scurtu (six victories).

One of the most intense combats between USAAF and ARR fighters took place on Saturday, 10 June 1944. In an effort to inflict decisive damage on the Ploiesti oilfields, 46 bomb-carrying P-38Js of the 82nd FG, escorted by a similar number of long-range Lightning fighters of the 1st FG, took off from Foggia, in Italy, before dawn – some two hours earlier than usual. However, their attempt to intrude into Rumania undetected was foiled by the *Freya* and *Würzburg* radar chain that picked up the faint signal of the low-flying formation prior to it entering Rumanian airspace. Thanks to this early warning, the 'Tiger' fighter command post alerted both Rumanian and

Slt av Vasile Cârciuvoianu (three victories – killed in a flying accident on 31 May 1944) gestures towards the scoreboard of his group commander, *Cpt av* Lucian Toma, marked on the white rudder of Bf 109G-2 'White 1', believed to be Wk-Nr. 14680. Each of the stripes is topped by a small red star, representing Toma's score at the time – all seven victories had been achieved during the ARR's first campaign. Relegated to home defence duties and various desk jobs, Toma would score no further kills until April 1944, when the USAAF started attacking Rumanian military and civilian objectives. Also pictured are, from left to right, *Adj av* Constantin 'Titi' Popescu (six victories), *Adj av* Alexandru Economu (five victories – killed in action on 26 July 1944) and *Adj stag av* Casian Teodorescu (three). All were members of *Escadrila 53 vânătoare, Grupul 7 vânătoare*

Groundcrewmen indicate damage to the radial engine of IAR 81C 'White 336' of *Slt av* Ioan Iatan, *Grupul 6 vânătoare*, which was inflicted by a P-38 Lightning on 18 May 1944. Note the enormous cannon shell exit hole in front of the cockpit, which punctured the main fuel tank. Luckily for the Rumanian pilot, the fuel level must have been low, as it was not ignited by the shell. He might otherwise have suffered the fate that awaited many IAR 80/81 pilots, who were burned alive when the flames were swept back to the cockpit by the airstream. *Slt av* Iatan claimed a P-38J on 10 June 1944, but was himself wounded in combat

Slt av Constantin Baltă poses near the tail of his IAR 81C. The two freshly-painted white victory bars on the rudder represent the pair of B-24s that Baltă downed on 6 May 1944. He was wounded by the second Liberator's gunners and was barely able to get home with the damaged 'White 372'. Baltă claimed his kills whilst serving as a flying instructor at the German-run fighter pilot school at Brasov (Brassó, Kronstadt). He and his comrades would regularly fly emergency sorties against USAAF aircraft which were attacking Brasov. He ended the war with two B-24s confirmed and another probable, earning him nine ARR victories

A *Grupul 6 vânătoare* pilot prepares to take off from Popesti-Leordeni airfield in 'White 369'. This particular aircraft was shot down over the airfield during the low-level dogfight of 10 June 1944 between IAR 81Cs of *Gr 6 vân* and P-38Js of the 71st FS, its pilot, *Lt av* Alexandru Nicolae D Limburg of *Escadrila 62 vânătoare*, nicknamed 'The General', being killed. He was one of three Rumanian pilots killed or posted as missing on this day. Note the three coloured (yellow?) triangles on the forward fuselage just above the port wing cannon, which were symbols of air or ground victories. These were not Limburg's, however, for he had not claimed a kill prior to his death

German units of the imminent attack. All combat-ready IAR 80/81s were hastily scrambled.

As the unsuspecting American pilots approached Popesti-Leordeni airfield, home of *Grupul 6 vânătoare*, at low level, they were bounced from above by the IAR fighters. Several Lightnings fell victim to the Rumanians' guns in that first pass, while others, trying to manoeuvre at low altitude, either hit the ground or the P-38 beside them. Only a few actually managed to engage the Rumanian fighters. To add to the carnage, the airfield's flak gunners were firing indiscriminately.

The defenders also suffered losses of their own, with two IAR 81Cs colliding in mid-air and a third fighter being hit by 'friendly' flak. Nevertheless, *Grupul 6 vânătoare* emerged as the clear winners of this mêlée, its 23 pilots claiming an identical number of P-38s destroyed. The CO of the unit, 34-year-old *Cpt av* Dan Vizanty (the top scoring IAR 80/81 pilot with a reported 43+ victories), added two Lightnings to his tally, while six other pilots also claimed 'doubles'. Three Rumanian pilots had been killed and a fourth gravely wounded.

The P-38Js of the 82nd FG faired little better than their counterparts in the 1st FG, as they too were bounced by Rumanian and German Bf 109Gs some distance from their target – the large *Româno-Americană* oil refinery. Five Lightnings were claimed by *Grupul 7 vânătoare*, and some 15 by Luftwaffe *Jagdfliegern* (notably I./JG 53 and III./JG 77) for the loss of one of their own, the Germans having scrambled 64 Bf 109Gs and two Fw 190s. A further five P-38s were reportedly shot down by the flak defences surrounding Ploiesti, and at least three other locations.

Eventually, ARR HQ reduced the total number of enemy aircraft confirmed destroyed on 10 June to 18 downed by fighters and seven by flak defences, with the destruction of three more being shared between gunners on the ground and Axis fighters.

Although Rumanian and German fighters and flak initially claimed double (51) the actual number of P-38s lost during this ill-fated mission, the loss of two-dozen USAAF aircraft (one quarter of the attacking formation) nevertheless represented a tremendous victory for the defenders. Indeed, it was the highest loss ratio for any mission flown by a significant number of P-38s in World War 2. In return, the Lightning pilots were themselves credited with 33 confirmed kills, six probables and eight damaged, as well as ten locomotives destroyed.

The actual Rumanian losses were 14 aircraft destroyed, with most of these being non-combat types surprised by US fighters whilst on their way to dispersal, or caught on the ground.

The *vânători*'s success did not last too long, however. Facing a technically and numerically superior enemy, they managed to shoot down fewer and fewer US aeroplanes, while losing an increasing number of their own. On 23 June, for example, the 36-year-old CO of the *élite Grupul 7 vânătoare*, *Căpitan aviator* Virgil Trandafirescu, lost his life in a dogfight with P-51s. During the same engagement, group mates and leading aces *Lt av* Teodor Greceanu and *Cpt av* Dan Scurtu were also downed, ending up in hospital. A number of other IAR 80/81 pilots, including *Căpitan comandor aviator* Ioan V Sandu, CO of *Grupul 1 vânătoare*, were lost on this day too. Sandu was the highest ranking ARR fighter pilot to be killed in combat, the wing commander reportedly being gunned down by USAAF fighters while descending in his parachute.

The death of two fighter group commanders (of the four involved in combat on this day) and the wounding of two experienced Messerschmitt pilots on the 23rd was a tremendous blow to the small Rumanian fighter force.

Twenty-four hours earlier, the ARR had celebrated the third anniversary of its involvement in action on the eastern front. By 22 June 1944, a total of 834 Soviet aircraft had been confirmed as shot down by Rumanian fighter pilots, bomber gunners and flak crews, with a further 143 counted as probables. The ARR had in turn lost 186 aeroplanes in combat with the VVS, along with 402 airmen killed, wounded or missing in action.

On 3 July, *Subsecretariatul de Stat al Aerului* (SSA, or the State's Sub-secretariat for Air Affaires) summed up the results of the past ten weeks of combat with the USAAF. On 4 April, when the first US attack on Rumania in 1944 was flown, there were 115 fighters available to oppose the raid. By 24 June, that number had been

Pilots of the IAR 81C-equipped *Grupul 6 vânătoare* run towards their aircraft, parked at Popesti-Leordeni airfield, near Bucharest, on 10 June 1944 in response to the alarm being sounded. Within the hour they had jumped the unsuspecting P-38Js of the 71st FS/1st FG, heading at low-level for the Ploiesti oilfields. Note the reversed white chevron painted on the fuselage of 'White 343', denoting that it was the personal mount of one of the *Grup's* three squadron commanders

USAAF aircraft started to appear over Rumania in significant numbers from 4 April 1944 onwards, and casualties among the *vânători* quickly mounted. The three IAR 80/81-equipped fighter groups (the 1st, 2nd and 6th) bore the brunt of the losses, and in a period of less than 20 weeks – known to Rumanian airmen as the 'American Campaign' – at least 32 IAR pilots were killed in action, including 11 aces. These losses exceeded total casualties suffered in the previous two-and-a-half years' fighting against the Soviets. Scenes similar to the one depicted here – a burning IAR 80, often with the pilot trapped in the blazing wreck after a combat sortie due to the faulty aft-sliding cockpit – became familiar

A group of *vânători* from *Grupul 9 vânātoare* gather beside Bf 109G-6 'Yellow 1', the personal aircraft of *Cpt av* Serbānescu, at Tecuci airfield, Moldavia, in late May 1944. The pilots are, from left, *Adj av* Emil Bālan (ten victories), *Lt av* Hariton Dusescu (12), Serbānescu (55), *Of ech cl. III av* Ioan Milu (52), *Adj av* Gheorghe Scordilā (two shared) and *Lt av* Teodor Greceanu (24+). Four of these pilots were shot down during the 'American Campaign', Serbānescu and Bālan being killed and Greceanu and Milu wounded

Lt av Gheorghe Popescu-Ciocānel started the war as a pilot in short-range reconnaissance squadron *Escadrila 19 observatie*, equipped with obsolete IAR 39 biplanes. While performing a low-level observation mission over Soviet-held Bessarabia on 19 June 1941, he had a brush with death when several I-16s jumped the lone biplane, riddling it with bullets which killed the observer and rear gunner. Although wounded, Popescu-Ciocānel shook off his attackers and crash-landed in friendly territory. At the end of the ARR's first campaign he transferred to the *vânātori*, returning to the eastern front in 1943. Promoted to *cāpitan aviator*, Popescu-Ciocānel became one of the unit's best pilots. His score had reached 17 by July, but on the 26th of that month he was one of seven pilots downed in combat with a formation of USAAF fighters. In this photo, taken pre-war, the officer wears an early version of the observer's badge (on the left) and an early airman's badge, both in King Carol II style

reduced to just 50. Aside from the huge losses in machinery, some 33 pilots had been killed in action.

The carnage continued on 28 June, when seven-victory IAR 80/81 ace *Cpt av* Parsifal Stefānescu of *Grupul 1 vânātoare* was shot down and killed by Mustangs. He would prove to be the last casualty suffered by the IAR 80/81 units in their uneven fight against the USAAF, as ARR HQ decided to effectively withdraw the obsolete indigenous fighter from the home defence force on 5 July. This left just the Bf 109G-equipped *Grupuri 7* and *9 vânātoare* to defend Rumania alongside Luftwaffe units, *Grupul 9 vânātoare* having been hastily recalled from the Soviet front. Its place was in turn taken by the IAR 80/81 *Grupuri*, who found the VVS fighters easier to deal with than USAAF P-38s and P-51s.

On 22 July, *Grupul 9 vânātoare* enjoyed one of its most successful days in combat with the Americans. The Messerschmitt pilots, led by their venerable commander, *Cāpitan aviator* Alexandru Serbānescu, took of from Tecuci at 1100 hrs to engage a mixed force of P-38s and P-51s heading for Bucharest, and then on to the USSR, as part of a shuttle raid. The Bf 109G pilots succeeded in surprising their American foes, and six P-38s were shot down without loss – an IAR 81C pilot of *Gr 1 vân* claimed a seventh Lightning. Fifteenth Air Force records for this date list only five P-38Js lost over Rumania.

However, when the USAAF fighter force flew back through Rumania from the USSR on the return leg of their shuttle raid, it was the Mustang pilots' who prevailed in combat. *Grupul 9 vânātoare* lost seven Bf 109G-6s of the seventeen that had been scrambled to engage what had erroneously been reported by the 'Tiger' fighter command

post as 'only 20 bombers with a weak fighter escort'. It turned out that the number of bombers was in fact much higher, and the 'weak fighter escort' comprised 100+ P-38s and P-51s!

Three ARR pilots were killed outright in the ensuing dogfight, while three others were wounded. All of these men were veterans of numerous aerial battles, and aces with many victories. Amongst those shot down was the deputy CO of *Grupul 9 vânātoare*, *Cpt av* Gheorghe Popescu-Ciocānel, who had achieved 19 victories. Baling out of his flaming fighter,

1944 – YEAR OF THE CRUCIBLE

Popescu-Ciocănel landed with severe wounds and died in hospital ten days later.

Grupul 9 vânătoare pilots claimed 11 USAAF aircraft shot down, although only two P-38Js appear on the Fifteenth Air Force loss lists. Another unofficial source states that 20 P-38s and ten P-51s were lost over Rumania, Ukraine and Poland on this day, and the latter data seems to be a little more accurate. Whatever the actual figure was, these results could not disguise the appalling losses inflicted on the élite *Grupul 9 vânătoare*. And the decimation of the unit continued on the very last day of July, when *Locotenent aviator* Dinu Florea Pistol, CO of *Esc 48 vân*, lost his life whilst attacking B-17s and B-24s.

Having claimed three kills prior to his demise, Pistol's death was particularly mourned by *Căpitan aviator* Alexandru Serbănescu, the battle-hardened CO of the group. Some years earlier, both men had switched to the *vânători* from the mountain troops, and then been posted together to *Grupul 7 vânătoare* on the Stalingrad front. Unknown to *Cpt av* Serbănescu, his time was also running out.

Eighteen days later, on 18 August 1944, Rumanian pilots took the fight to the Americans for the last time. Thirteen Bf 109G-6s of *Grupul 9 vânătoare* rendezvoused with twelve *Gustavs* of *Grupul 7 vânătoare* over Buzău. Minutes later, they were joined by 21 Luftwaffe fighters, making a total force of 46 Bf 109Gs. This was the sum total of Axis fighters available to defend Rumania.

Shortly after the two ARR groups took off, *Sectorul 2 vânătoare* (2nd Fighter Sector) radioed the Rumanian pilots and instructed them to intercept a larger force of USAAF fighters in the vicinity of Brasov, above the Carpathian Mountains. The Bf 109Gs clashed with the P-51s at a height of 7500 m (24,600 ft), which was practically the combat ceiling for the Bf 109G-6. As usual, the Mustangs outnumbered the joint Rumanian-German formation by at least two-to-one, and to make matters worse, the Americans attacked the Messerschmitts from above. Within minutes the outcome of the fight had been decided. Amongst the first to fall was 32-year-old *Căpitan aviator* Alexandru Serbănescu, then leading ARR ace with 55 victories achieved in 590 combat sorties.

Adjutant aviator **Alexandru Moldoveanu spent his fighter pilot career, spanning the entire war, in the Bf 109-equipped *Grupul 7 vânătoare*. On 29 June 1943, during a low-level dogfight with Yaks near Tschaltye, he collided with one of them, sending it crashing to the ground. Luckily for the Rumanian, only the starboard wing of his Bf 109G was damaged, so he was able to return to Mariupol airfield, in the Ukraine. Moldoveanu fought his last aerial battle on 10 August 1944, when he clashed with Fifteenth Air Force Mustangs near Bucharest and belly-landed his damaged *Gustav* without injury. He finished the war with nine aerial victories**

This heavily camouflaged Bf 109G-6 is parked in a 'sand box' on a Moldavian airfield in early August 1944, such a revetment giving the fighter a modicum of protection from strafing USAAF and VVS aircraft. Note the unusual black spiral painted on the white spinner

Recently-graduated *Slt av* Vasile Gavriliu shows off his new uniform as he walks past *Grupul 7 vânătoare's* Bf 109Es in April 1942. Note that the *Emils* still display slanted white victory bars from the 1941 campaign behind their respective air intakes. 'Chitzu' Gavriliu emerged as one of the most effective Rumanian Messerschmitt pilots, claiming some 27 victories, which placed him ninth in the ARR's unofficial list of aces. His successes included a dozen victories achieved against German and Hungarian aircraft (mostly transports destroyed on the ground), making him the top-scoring anti-Axis fighter pilot of Rumania's 'Western Front' campaign

Flying with a faulty radio, Serbănescu failed to hear the warnings being shouted to him by his colleagues that a Mustang was manoeuvring onto his tail. His wingman, *Adj stag av* Traian Dârjan, who was flying some 350 ft off his right wing, watched on helplessly as a red-nosed P-51 (almost certainly from the 31st FG) fell in behind *Cpt av* Serbănescu's Bf 109G-6 'Yellow 1' and opened fire. With Serbănescu probably already dead, the Messerschmitt dove vertically and disintegrated when it hit the ground near Brasov.

Another outstanding officer, and 14-victory ace, *Lt av* Vasile Gavriliu, was more fortunate when he force-landed his damaged fighter just minutes later – at least 50 holes had been punched through its fuselage and wings. The Germans also suffered a terrible mauling, with at least three Bf 109Gs being destroyed and one pilot killed. In return, Major Jürgen Harder of I./JG 53 claimed the destruction of a P-51, which proved to be the sole victory scored by the Axis pilots on this day.

The loss of *Cpt av* Serbănescu effectively signalled the end of the defence of Rumania by the ARR, for the next day a dispersal order arrived from Bucharest instructing pilots not to engage USAAF formations any more. Instead, the remnants of the fighter force would be transferred from Buzău to the quiet of Mamaia, on the shores of the Black Sea. Only German fighters would now oppose American aircraft over Rumania, taking the fight to the Allies until war's end.

The dispersal order for *Grupul 9 vânătoare* was resented by its surviving pilots, who viewed it as a cowardly climb down in the face of the enemy. 'The Group ran away', *Lt av* Dobran bitterly recorded in his wartime diary.

According to the author's research, Rumania was subjected to 42 daylight raids by the USAAF and at least 23 nocturnal raids by the RAF in 1944. Rumanian documents state that the USAAF lost a total of 223 bombers and 36 fighters during the course of these missions, with 56 bombers being shot by fighters, 131 brought down by flak and 36 lost to other causes. The Americans lost 15 fighters in aerial combat, one to flak and 20 to other causes. Official Allied losses in terms of personnel amounted to approximately 2200 airmen. The total Allied aircraft attrition rate over Rumania was approximately seven per cent, compared to an average of 3.5 per cent over Western Europe. ARR losses were also heavy, with more than 80 fighters being destroyed in combat. The *Jagdwaffe* suffered slightly fewer losses.

CHANGING SIDES

On the morning of 20 August 1944, a powerful Soviet offensive opened in the Iasi-Chisināu (Jassy-Kishinev) sector of the eastern front. By the afternoon, the ill-equipped and outnumbered Rumanian-German ground defence had virtually collapsed in the face of an attack supported by a large number of VVS assault aircraft and fighters. Desperate to halt the Red Army's advance into Rumanian territory, the ARR and the Luftwaffe committed all available aircraft. Even so, the VVS could muster two-and-a-half times more machines – of the 1952 Soviet aircraft stationed in the southern sector, 802 were fighters, and this total did not include the Black Sea Fleet. Opposing them were no more than 300 Axis fighters, of which only 250 were combat-worthy.

Alongside the Bf 109Gs of *Grupul 9 vânātoare* were the IAR 80/81-equipped units, which had been withdrawn from the defence of the homeland, where they were considered too vulnerable to face superior US fighters. They fared little better against the Soviets, however, for on 20 and 21 August five IAR 81Cs of *Grupul 2 vânātoare* were lost. The unit did manage to claim a La-5FN and two La-7s confirmed as shot down, plus an Airacobra listed as a probable. *Gr 9 vân* did somewhat better, though, reporting ten aircraft downed during the two days.

The Messerschmitt pilots also sustained casualties, with two Bf 109G-6s falling to La-5FNs over Moldavia on the 22nd. One of the downed pilots was 17-victory ace *Adj stag av* Traian Dârjan, who was briefly captured by Soviet troops. The other *Gustav* pilot shot down was five-victory ace *Adj stag av* Costin Miron, who landed safely in Rumanian-held territory. Two IAR 81s of *Gr 4 vân* and a third from *Gr 2 vân* were also lost in combat. Only one victory claim was filed. Besides these combat losses, two unserviceable IAR 80/81s were destroyed on the ground at Leipzig airfield by retreating German troops.

By 23 August 1944 it became clear that the war was lost. That evening King Michael made a radio broadcast in which he announced that armistice terms had been sought from the Allies. Hostilities against the USSR would stop at 0400 hrs the next morning. The King's announcement took German forces in Rumania completely by surprise, and they

Adj stag av Vasile Ionitã (left) and *Adj av* Stefan Nica (right) of *Grupul 2 vânãtoare* prepare for a combat mission against Soviet aircraft at Gherãesti-Bacãu airfield, in Moldavia, on 10 August 1944. By this time IAR 80/81-equipped units were forbidden to engage the USAAF because of the type's inferiority to American fighters. Indeed, not one P-51 combat kill was ever attributed to an IAR 80/81 pilot. The aircraft were moved instead to the Soviet front, where they faced an enemy considered to be less dangerous. Ionitã scored a confirmed and a probable kill over B-24s, representing six victories, while Nica downed two Soviet I-16s in 1941

Adj stag rez av Traian Dârjan poses
in front of his Bf 109G. The young
NCO was the favourite wingman of
many leading officer-pilots, notably
Cpt av Gheorghe Popescu-Ciocănel
of *Grupul 9 vânătoare*. He was shot
down by La-5s on the penultimate
day of fighting between Rumania
and the Soviets whilst at the
controls of Bf 109G-6 'Yellow 6'
Wk-Nr. 163580, but he escaped from
captivity and returned to his unit on
30 September 1944

continued fighting. Indeed, the situation between the former allies deteriorated rapidly, and that afternoon ARR fighters intercepted transport aircraft carrying reinforcements to the *Wehrmacht*. Rumanian flak also opened fire on German aircraft, and the day after the armistice, *Cpt av* Lucian-Eduard Toma, CO of *Gr 7 vân*, scored the first Rumanian success over the Luftwaffe when he shot down a troop-carrying Ju 52/3m over Boteni airfield.

Earlier that day, *Lt av* Stefan Florescu of *Esc 53 vân* became the last Rumanian fighter pilot to shoot down a Soviet aircraft when he destroyed a Pe-2 in the Mamaia zone. Once the Soviets gained control of Rumania, Florescu was hunted by Red Army authorities, although they did not find him. His kill was achieved with a Bf 109E, and almost certainly represents the final combat victory attributed to this model of Messerschmitt.

On 25 August 1944 Rumania declared war on its former allies, Germany and Hungary. Fighter pilots defending the capital were no longer confused about the identity of their new enemy, and as if to prove the point, six Luftwaffe bombers (He 111Hs of I./KG 4 and Ju 87Ds of I./SG 2) were reportedly downed by Bf 109Gs of *Grupuri 7* and *9 vânătoare*, with another four damaged. *Adj ad* Gheorghe Grecu of *Gr 4 vân*, flying IAR 81C 'White 394', also downed a six-engined Me 323 *Gigant* and a Ju 52/3m, both of which were carrying reinforcements. Under the ARR's scoring system, Grecu was credited with five aerial victories to become Rumania's final 'ace-in-a-day'!

Clashes between the former allies continued near Bucharest, with Rumanian fighters downing nine Luftwaffe aircraft, eight of which fell to *Grupul 9 vânătoare* – two Me 323 *Giganten*, Ju 52/3ms, Bf 109Gs and Bf 110Fs, with another four probables. Still more were destroyed on the ground. *Lt av* Vasile Gavriliu also added to his score that day with an He 111H and a Ju 52/3m shot down over Bucharest, plus two further Junkers transports and a Junkers W 34 set on fire on the ground. He was credited with a record nine victories, but Gavriliu's day ended when his Bf 109G-6 was hit by ground fire, causing him to effect a force landing. These air and ground kills, together with other post-23 August victories, gave Gavriliu a total of 12 victories (mostly transport aircraft destroyed on the ground). This tally made him the most successful anti-Axis ARR ace.

There were losses too, but mainly of aircraft destroyed on their bases or captured by the Germans. Some were even seized by Soviet troops who were generally not behaving like allies. Several Rumanian fighter pilots were killed in combat with the Luftwaffe, including *Adj stag av* Constantin Stolică of *Gr 7 vân*, whose yellow-crossed Bf 109G-6 was shot down by a black-crossed Bf 109G-6 over Căldărusani on 28 August. Another Bf 109G-6 of *Gr 6 vân* (Wk-Nr. 166167, with no fuselage number) had previously been shot down by 'friendly' flak. It crashed into Bucharest's Lake Floreasca, killing novice pilot, *Adj av* Constantin Anastasiu. Several more Rumanian *Gustavs* sustained combat damage, but without further loss of life.

On 31 August the Red Army entered Bucharest. By this time the last German troops had withdrawn from Rumania into Hungarian Transylvania and Bulgaria. Those captured by the Rumanians were handed over to the Soviets, including wounded Luftwaffe airmen seized in their hospital beds.

By the time the fighting stopped, 22 German aircraft had been claimed by ARR in aerial battles, with another five set on fire on the ground. Only four Rumanian aircraft were acknowledged as having been shot down by the Luftwaffe, with another 30 destroyed on the ground or captured. The real losses, however, were significantly higher.

THE TRANSYLVANIAN CAMPAIGN

On 6 September, the newly re-formed *Corpul 1 Aerian Român* (C1AR) ordered its aircraft – freshly repainted with the old tricolour cockades adopted as pro-Allied national markings – to the so-called 'western front' to confront Axis forces. These aircraft moved from bases around Bucharest and Wallachia north-west over the Transylvanian Alps to new airfields in Rumanian-held southern Transylvania. There, they were to provide air support for the joint Soviet-Rumanian offensive against Hungarian and German troops defending northern Transylvania.

Three fighter groups were attached to C1AR, namely the Bf 109-equipped mixed *Grupul 7/9 vânătoare* (*Escadrile 47, 48* and *56*) with 27 aircraft, and the IAR 80/81-equipped *Grupul 2 vânătoare* (*Escadrile 65* and *66*) and *Grupul 6 vânătoare* (*Escadrile 59, 61* and *62*), totalling 57 aircraft. These were supplemented by nine IAR 80s and six Bf 109Gs of the independent *Escadrila 44 vânătoare*, the first Rumanian fighter unit to arrive at the front on 5 September. The nine *escadrile* fielded 99 fighters, representing approximately two-thirds of the total combat strength of the expeditionary air force. VVS fighter and bomber regiments were also deployed to airfields in the region.

The ARR's first official day of operations against Axis forces in the new theatre was 7 September. *Escadrila 44 vânătoare*, the only combat-ready fighter element, had to fly all the fighter sorties, despite a limited number of aircraft and a lack of experienced pilots. Yet, *Esc 44 vân* put up 20 aircraft to fly four missions. The first against the enemy was conducted by two IAR 80 *patrule*, their task being reconnaissance over the new front and low-level attack against enemy vehicle columns. Although they had instructions to avoid contact with enemy aircraft, two clashes were still recorded.

The first encounter involved six IAR 80/81s and eight Fw 190Fs of 4./SG 2 north of Sibiu (known as Nagyszeben to the Hungarians and Hermannstadt to the Germans). Aircraft 'White 292', flown by *Adj stag av* Nicolae Zaharia, was shot down in flames over Rumanian-controlled territory and the wounded pilot rescued.

The morning of 8 September saw the bulk of C1AR *vânători* fly into their new forward base at Turnisor (Kistorony/Neppendorf), close to Sibiu, where C1AR had established its headquarters.

On that first day of operations, one Rumanian Messerschmitt pilot was lost when *Adj stag av* Gheorghe Buholtzer, flying Bf 109G-6 'Yellow 8' (which was reportedly still carrying the old 'Michael's Cross' national markings and yellow Axis identification colours), was shot down on landing by an over-zealous female Soviet flak gunner. This was only the first of a series of fatal incidents in which Soviet flak

Sitting astride the engine of his Bf 109G-6 is *Slt av* Stefan Octavian Ciutac of *Grupul 9 vânătoare*, an ace with 11 victories. All his victims were USAAF aircraft except for a Luftwaffe Gotha Go 242 transport glider destroyed on 15 September 1944 while parked at Cluj-Someseni – this photograph was taken at the airfield on 27 October 1944 in front of the ruined hangars, which had been demolished by the retreating Germans. On 19 September 'Kiki' Ciutac had been bounced by a Luftwaffe Bf 109G *Rotte* over Alba Iulia, in southern Transylvania, compelling him to bale out his burning Bf 109G-6 'Blue 3' (Wk-Nr. 166012). Unteroffizier Tammen of 6./JG 52 claimed two Rumanian *Gustavs* that day, his other victim being *Slt av* Andrei Popa, whose Bf 109G-6 ('Red 9' Wk-Nr. 166135) was hit in the radiator during combat. Popa duly belly-landed on Drâmbari airfield

crews erroneously (or deliberately) shot down German-built aircraft flown by Rumanian pilots, who had been their enemies just a few weeks earlier. Generally, relations between the Soviets and the Rumanians remained tense.

15 September saw a daring mission flown by pilots of *Grupul 9 vânătoare*, the unit being sent to neutralise Axis aircraft at Szamosfalva (Someseni) airfield, north of Kolozsvár (Cluj), the capital of Transylvania. Six of the most experienced flyers volunteered for the surprise low-level attack, the mission being led by *Lt av* Vasile Gavriliu, the ARR's top ace in the campaign against the Axis. The Bf 109Gs took off from Turnisor and headed north, and after making a 180-degree turn, they approached the target from the north so as to take the flak defences by surprise. Flying at low level, the six pilots strafed the airfield in a single pass. *Lt av* Dobran set a Hungarian Reggiane Re.2000 *Héja* fighter on fire, while Gavriliu claimed a twin-engined Focke-Wulf Fw 58 *Weihe*. Three German transport gliders (probably Gotha Go 242s) and a few trucks were also destroyed during the attack. All the Rumanian aircraft returned unscathed.

As the battle for Transylvania grew in intensity, more and more missions were ordered. Both sides relied heavily on their air power, although ARR and Luftwaffe fighter pilots tried to avoid confrontation. There are even unconfirmed reports of Rumanian and German Messerschmitt pilots – comrades-in-arms not so long ago – flying side-by-side above the front, with their radio sets turned off, exchanging the traditional *'Hals-und Beinbruch'* greeting.

All displays of friendship ended on 16 September when one of six IAR 81Cs of *Gr 2 vân* fell victim to a Bf 109G *Rotte* from 6./JG 52 near Kolozsvár (Cluj). The aircraft ('White 413'), flown by *Adj stag av* Iosif Chiuhulescu – a six-victory ace – was sent down in a spin after the first firing pass made by the experienced Unteroffizier Heinrich Tammen, who would subsequently shoot down ten ARR aircraft in less than two weeks. In fact Tammen's score of Rumanian aircraft in this period exceeded that officially credited to the ARR's entire fighter force for the entire eight-month-long western campaign!

Flak also caused significant losses among the strafing Rumanian fighters, two IAR 81s

of *Grupul 2 vânatoare* being hit north of Nyárádfö (Ungheni) and crashing into the Mures (Maros/Mieresch) river on 18 September. Both pilots, *Slt av* Nicolae Smeianu and his wingman *Adj stag* Dumitru Marinescu, who had previously been credited with two victories, were killed.

The following day, Bf 109s from both sides clashed for the first time in the skies over Transylvania. Two Luftwaffe Bf 109Gs engaged five similar aircraft from *Grupul 9 vânatoare*, and the Germans came out on top. *Slt av* Andrei Pop's 'Red 9' (Wk-Nr. 166135) suffered hits in its radiator and he was forced to land at Drâmbari (Dombár) emergency airfield, while *Slt av* Stefan *'Kiki'* Ciutac, an experienced 11-victory *vânator*, baled out of his burning 'Blue 3' (Wk-Nr. 166012) near Alba Iulia (Gyulafehérvár/Weissburg). Both *Gustavs* were further victims of Unteroffizier Tammen. The third Rumanian loss was 'Red 5' (Wk-Nr. 166210), which crashed on take off, killing *Slt rez av* Prince Gheorghe Brâncoveanu.

The decimated *Escadrila 44 vânatoare* was ordered home on 20 September, by which time its strength had been reduced to 15 fighters. *Grupul 2 vânatoare* (14 IAR 80/81s), *Grupul 6 vânatoare* (11 IAR 80/81s) and *Grupul 9 vânatoare* (17 Bf 109Gs) remained at the front.

BLOODBATH OVER TURDA

On 22 September, a joint Soviet-Rumanian offensive opened in the Turda (Torda/Thorenburg) region, supported by ARR and VVS aircraft. The Luftwaffe was up in force, and Bf 109Gs and Fw 190s repeatedly attacked the Rumanian formations. While they could not intercept ARR Ju 88As thanks to the escorting Bf 109Gs, Luftwaffe fighters succeeded in getting amongst a formation of Hs 129Bs escorted by IAR 81s, shooting down one of each type.

Activity peaked on 23 September with three aerial battles over Turda involving up to 40 aircraft. In the morning, during their second mission, two IAR 81Cs of *Escadrila 59 vânatoare* clashed with six to eight Fw 190s. *Slt av* Petre Mihăilescu, a pilot credited with nine victories, was killed when the fuel tank of his IAR 81 was hit and exploded. More IARs of *Grupul 6 vânatoare*, as well as Bf 109Gs of II./JG 52, then joined the battle, and a further two IAR 80s and an ARR Bf 109G-6 were soon shot down, one pilot being killed and the others wounded. The IARs fell victim to Feldwebel Willi Maaßen and Leutnant Martin Ludwig of 5. and 6./JG 52, while the Bf 109G was yet another victim of Unteroffizier Tammen.

The Rumanians, too, claimed victories, with single Bf 109Gs being credited to *Lt av* Dumitru *'Take'* Baciu of *Grupul 6 vânatoare* and *Adj av* Stavăr (Stavarache) Androne of *Grupul 2 vânatoare*, while an Fw 190F was downed by *Adj av* Dumitru *'Mitică'* Chera of *Grupul 6 vânatoare*. Chera and

Still in the cockpit of his IAR 81C, *Lt av* Dan Stefănescu of *Grupul 6 vânatoare* describes the aerial battle he has just fought against USAAF aircraft in the summer of 1944. Despite the gestures, Stefănescu is not known to have scored any victories prior to his death in combat fighting Luftwaffe Fw 190s over Transylvania on 22 September 1944

Wearing a fashionable black shirt and matching tie, topped by a white service cap, and displaying his *Virtutea Aeronautică cu Spade* decoration, *Adj av* Dumitru Chera smiles for a comrade's camera in early 1944. Initially fighting with the IAR 80/81-equipped *Grupul 1 vânătoare*, 'Mitică' Chera downed three Liberators, and shared a fourth with his patrol. After Rumania changed sides, he added a Luftwaffe Bf 109G to his score on 23 September – only three such claims were made by IAR 80/81 pilots. He also destroyed an He 111H and an Fw 190 on the ground, although these victories were not officially sanctioned. Chera's final official score totalled 13 victories

Baciu also claimed another Bf 109G each, but these were not filed officially.

Although the three aerial victories reported by the Rumanian fighter pilots were also mentioned in a rare Soviet assessment of the joint VVS-ARR air activity in Cluj area, only one Fw 190F, of I./SG 2, can actually be found in German documents as having been damaged that day. There is no trace in *Verlustmeldungen* (Luftwaffe loss reports) of any Bf 109Gs being shot down on the 23rd. However, Oberfähnrich Gerhard Messner of 5./JG 52 is reported as having being killed in his Bf 109G-6 'Black 4' (Wk-Nr. 166014) over an unspecified location in Rumania on 24 September – the day's discrepancy in the records may not be significant.

Regardless of the facts, the claim by the ARR of three enemy aircraft destroyed on 23 September for the loss of five is regarded by Rumanian historians as a unique 'triumph' for IAR 80 pilots fighting the Luftwaffe and Hungarian air force in the skies over Transylvania.

Combat resumed over Turda on 25 September. At 1000 hrs eight IAR 80/81s of *Grupul 2 vânătoare* took off to escort Rumanian bombers and attack aircraft, and to patrol the region. Followed by further IARs of *Grupul 6 vânătoare*, they were soon confronted by Luftwaffe fighters. Several overlapping aerial battles developed involving 50 aircraft – numbers not seen by the Rumanians since the USAAF raids.

Rumanian documents record four clashes over Turda between Rumanian and German aircraft, with six Hs 129Bs of *Grupul 8 asalt* engaging six Bf 109Gs, eight IAR 80s of *Grupul 2 vânătoare* attacking five Bf 109Gs, another eight IAR 80s of *Grupul 2 vânătoare* opposing six Bf 109Gs and ten IAR 80s of *Grupul 6 vânătoare* tackling six Bf 109Gs. Despite the Rumanians' numerical superiority, the IARs again provided little opposition for the experienced Luftwaffe pilots, and the combat turned into a real bloodbath. Six IARs were shot down and three pilots killed, namely *Lt av* Ioan Ivanciovici (11 victories), *Adj stag av* Franz Secicar (an ethnic German from Transylvania, who was credited with two victories) and *Adj sef av* Androne, who had claimed a German Bf 109G destroyed just two days earlier.

Among the victors was Leutnant Peter Düttmann of 6./JG 52, who, in the space of 12 minutes, had accounted for three IAR 80s to take his total score to 103. The other pilots to claim victories were Feldwebel Maaßen, Unteroffizier Tammen and an unidentified member of 3./SG 121. In contrast to the previous major clash, not one German fighter was claimed by the *vânători*. But the day was not yet over.

Shortly after noon, *Cpt av* Lucian Toma, CO of *Grupul 9 vânătoare* and an experienced fighter pilot with at least 11 victories, took off from Turnisor on a free hunt. Flying at 13,100 ft, he and his wingman, *Lt av* Ion Dobran, spotted a high-flying Ju 188 reconnaissance aircraft and climbed to engage it at 25,600 ft. Flying Bf 109G-6 'White 1', Toma opened fire at close range, and soon the Junkers started belching thick smoke. Toma continued to follow the German machine as it dived, and Dobran watched in horror as both hunter and prey hit the ground just a few feet apart. No trace of any parachute could be seen.

Cpt av Lucian Toma, CO of *Grupul 7/9 vânătoare* on the so-called 'Western Front', lights up a cigarette while waiting for the signal to take off in Bf 109G-6 'White 1' Wk-Nr. 165662. This was his personal aircraft, and he was subsequently killed in it by the rear gunner of a Luftwaffe Ju 188 that he was attacking over Cluj/Kolozsvár on 25 September 1944 – his first combat sortie on the new front. By then Toma had scored at least 11 victories, to which two more were posthumously added for the destruction of the Ju 188

Dobran's Bf 109G 'Blue 1' landed back at base and taxied to a stop near the tent housing the group's headquarters. The pilot slowly climbed out the cockpit and uttered just three words – 'Toma has fallen'. It was a repetition of the scene from five weeks earlier. Then, Dobran had announced the loss of Serbănescu, another captain, and leader from the same fighter group, who had been shot down in front of him.

The 33-year-old Toma had died on his first combat sortie against the new enemy, just seconds after shooting down the Luftwaffe reconnaissance aircraft. He was the last of seven ARR fighter group commanders to be killed in action during the war.

The next day was wet and cloudy, with visibility down to a few feet. But the weather was not the reason for Bucharest's order for all

ARR officer-pilots gather for a group photo in front of an IAR 81C at Turnisor (Kistorony, Neppendorf) airfield, near Sibiu (Nagyszeben, Hermannstadt), in southern Transylvania, in early October 1944. They are, from left to right, *Slt av* Mircea 'Shoto' Teodorescu (six victories), *Lt av* Dumitru 'Take' Baciu (ten plus three unconfirmed), *Lt av* Gheorghe Posteucă (two), *Cpt av* Dan-Valentin 'Mon Cher' Vizanty (43+), *Cpt av* Constantin 'Bâzu' Cantacuzino (69), *Cpt av* Traian Gavriliu (four) and *Lt av* Mircea 'Bébé' Dumitrescu (13)

IAR 80/81s to be grounded, pending a full assessment of the recent combat that had taken place. What had to be considered was that in the last four days the two groups equipped with the type had lost 11 aircraft in clashes with the Luftwaffe – almost a third of the total number of serviceable IARs! A decision was not long in arriving. The type was to be relegated to close support missions, providing air cover for Soviet ground units. From now on only the Bf 109Gs would be assigned the fighter role. The decimated *Gr 6 vân* was recalled and the surviving IAR 80/81s reassigned to *Gr 2 vân*, which was now the only frontline *Grup* equipped with the indigenous fighter. There was an initiative to re-equip IAR groups with Soviet Lavochkin La-5FNs and Yakovlev Yak-9s, but this plan failed in the face of Soviet reluctance.

At the end of September the results of the first month of the so-called 'western campaign' were assessed. *Grupul 2 vânătoare* had flown 60 missions (328 sorties), *Grupul 6 vânătoare* 77 missions (327 sorties) and *Grupul 9 vânătoare* 73 missions (314 sorties). A total of 105 Rumanian aircraft had been involved in 17 aerial battles with the Luftwaffe. Besides the four aircraft destroyed on the ground at Kolozsvár-Szamosfalva airfield, the *vânători* were credited with shooting down just four Luftwaffe machines. In contrast, ARR losses to enemy aircraft and flak had been high, totalling 25 fighters and 12 pilots dead. It had been a grim month for the *vânători*.

IN PURSUIT OF THE ENEMY

Bad weather and poor morale reduced the number of sorties flown during October. Most missions were to provide air cover for bombers and ground troops, although the occasional strafing raid was flown. Meteorological and tactical reconnaissance sorties were also frequent.

Pilots of Bf 109-equipped *Grupul 9 vânătoare* take a 'smoke break' on the tarmac of Cluj-Someseni (Kolozsvár-Szamosfalva in Hungarian) airfield before a combat mission over German-Hungarian lines in western Transylvania on 27 October 1944. In the centre, squadron CO *Lt av* Teodor Greceanu is standing with his left hand in the pocket of his German-issue trousers. Above and to the right of his pilot's badge he wears the *Mihai Viteazul* Order. Just weeks earlier some of these pilots had strafed Someseni/Szamosfalva airfield, destroying several Luftwaffe and MKHL (Royal Hungarian Air Force) aircraft parked on the very runway on which they are now standing. Note the tri-colour cockade, visible on the Bf 109G-6's underwing surface and fuselage side, this marking being adopted by the ARR after Rumania had changed sides

Enemy aerial activity was negligible, so there was little opportunity for air combat. Nevertheless, on the 9th Bf 109G-6 'Red 8' (Wk-Nr. 166061) of *Grupul 9 vânătoare* was reported missing. It is likely that the pilot, *Adj av* Ioan Vanca, had defected to the Germans. After the war he reputedly emigrated to the USA.

Bad weather continued for most of November. The fighter units had moved to a new landing ground in central Hungary, which was reduced to a sea of mud for most of the time, so combat sorties were rare. Losses continued, but the main causes were the weather and accidents on the unsuitable runways.

Despite the lack of activity, two unusual events were reported during this period. A Luftwaffe loss report dated 13 November lists Unteroffizier Uwe Rossen of 2./JG 53, flying Bf 109G-14 'Black 2' (Wk-Nr. 510880), as missing after an attack by an unidentified Bf 109G near Szolnok, close to the Rumanian base. There is no mention of any victory in *Grupul 9 vânătoare's* records for the period between October 1944 and January 1945. The most likely explanation is that the German airman was shot down by a VVS fighter, although the possibility remains that the reported assailant was a either a captured aircraft or one 'loaned' to the Soviets by the Rumanians. And although C1AR records show no combat missions for 4 December due to the weather, Hungarian documents mention the loss of an Fw 190F of the Hungarian 102 *Vadászbombázó-osztály* (102nd Fighter-Bomber Group), shot down over Börgönd airfield by what was described as a 'Rumanian-marked Bf 109G'. This again may have been a Messerschmitt flown by a Soviet pilot.

Despite the muddy landing strip, the *vânători* continued to obey orders and attempt take offs. The result was that over several days seven Bf 109Gs – a third of the group's available strength - were destroyed or damaged in taxiing accidents. Regardless of these senseless losses, the Soviets insisted on sending the Rumanian fighters over the frontline, justifying their orders by the intensity of enemy air activity, and by a desperate need to support Soviet and Rumanian troops trapped around Eger. Accordingly, there were further accidents, with little actually achieved. On 13 December the missions were finally called off.

Rumanian historians consider 19 December 1944 as the final day of the ARR's Hungarian campaign. It officially stared on 26 October, and is taken to include events inside the post-war borders of Hungary. In 54 days, the two fighter groups recorded only 25 missions (79 sorties). No aerial victories were claimed, and all losses were caused either by accidents during take off and landing or by flak.

When the Czechoslovakian campaign opened, the *Comandamentul aviatiei de vânătoare* (Fighter Aviation Command) reported 28 IAR 80/81s on the strength of *Grupul 2 vânătoare*, with *Grupul 9 vânătoare* having 27 Bf 109G-6s, of which 23 were serviceable.

By year's end, the Luftwaffe and the Hungarian air force remained active in the area, although less intensively than before because of a shortage of fuel. Nevertheless, a few missions were still flown over north-eastern Hungary, where Rumanian aircraft were operating. On 23 December, while escorting Ju 87D-5 Stukas of *Escadrila 74 picaj* to

Adj av **Ioan Mălăcescu acted as a reliable wingman to many leading ARR officer aces, and he also scored a considerable number of victories while watching his leaders' backs. His final flight took place on 13 December 1944, when he was severely wounded in an accident while taking off from the muddy airstrip at Túrkeve airfield, in Hungary. His Bf 109G 'Blue 3' Wk-Nr. 165135 (formerly of I./JG 27) was a write-off. Mălăcescu ended the war with 21 victories**

According to surviving ARR Messerschmitt pilots, it appears that *Lt av* Constantin 'Reazã' Rosariu was one of the most colourful personalities among the *vânãtori*, being a man who liked jokes, parties and women. He was also an outstanding fighter pilot and an excellent shot. He ended the war with a remarkable 33 victories against the Soviets, Americans and Germans, achieving ace status in combat with all three. His final score placed him fifth in the unofficial ARR list of aces. Here, Rosariu is casually seated on the cockpit sill of his Bf 109G, the fighter being parked somewhere on the eastern front during the summer of 1943. *Getta* was probably the name of his girlfriend at the time. Note the absence of a fuel cap for the spine tank (extreme right), and the effect of fuel spillage on the unusual mottled green camouflage paint

Poltár, an ARR Bf 109G *patrulã* was engaged by a *Kette* of black-crossed Bf 109Gs. During the ensuing combat, Rumanian Bf 109G-6 'White 1', usually flown by the group commander, but piloted that day by eight-victory ace *Adj av* Ioan Marinciu, was shot down and crashed near Zvolen (Zólyom, Altsohl). The wounded pilot ended up in the local hospital. The next day, two IAR 80As ('White 133' and 'White 144') were lost, the first to an Axis Bf 109G and the second to flak at Vadna, 16 miles from the Miskolc base. Finally, the fifth ranking ARR ace, *Lt av* Constantin *'Reazã'* Rosariu, in Bf 109G-6 'Blue 6' (Wk-Nr. 164997) was also hit by flak and forced down behind Russian lines. This was to be the last major activity for almost two months.

At least one IAR 80 and one of the Bf 109s shot down in air combat on 23/24 December can probably be attributed to Bf 109Gs of the *Magyar Királyi Honvéd Légierö* (MKHL, Royal Hungarian Home Defence Air Force) and its 101 *Puma Vadászezred* (101st *Puma* Fighter Wing), based at Veszprém airfield, north of Lake Balaton. On 22 December, *Szakaszvezetö* (Sgt) Lajos Krascsenics reportedly shot down a 'strangely-painted' Bf 109G which acted in a hostile manner. At about the same time, a radial-engined fighter with a yellow cowling was also reportedly downed by a Hungarian pilot. This was probably an IAR 80/81, as there is evidence of aircraft still serving in the frontline with yellow-painted engine cowlings as late as April 1945.

Between 7 September and 31 December 1944, the IAR-equipped squadrons had flown 814 sorties during the course of 167 missions (18 reconnaissance, 36 bomber escort, 103 ground support, nine low-level attack and one free-hunt). Over the same period the Messerschmitt-equipped *Grup* reported 551 sorties during 153 missions (32 reconnaissance, 84 bomber escort, four ground support, 30 low-level strafing and seven free-hunts).

C1AR crews had fought 25 aerial battles with German and Hungarian aircraft, IAR 80/81 pilots claiming just three victories for the loss of 17 aircraft (nine in combat, six to flak, one force-landed in enemy territory and one lost to other causes). The Bf 109G pilots had been credited with one air and five ground victories. Their losses were nine – four in combat, two to flak, one force-landed and two to other causes. Together with 26 fighters officially written-off, many others were so badly damaged that they had to go back to the IAR factory at Brasov for repair, removing them from combat for the rest of war.

THE FINAL YEAR BEGINS

As 1944 gave way to 1945, one thing remained unchanged – the weather. The conditions which had kept the Rumanian fighter force on the ground for much of the preceding months continued into the New Year. As a result, there was little action during January apart from weather reconnaissance flights. In mid-February *Grupul 9 vânătoare* moved from Miskolc, Hungary, to Lucenec (Losonc) airfield, in Slovakia, which had recently been vacated by the

enemy. There, it was joined by the newly-formed *Grupul 1 vânătoare* (*Escadrile 61* and *64*). This was essentially a scaled-down fighter group which had previously operated IAR 81s, but was now equipped with factory-fresh IAR-assembled Bf 109Gas, supplemented by older *Gustavs*, including a few refurbished machines captured from the Luftwaffe. The unit, however, arrived late. Its pilots were not fully trained, and the initial establishment comprised only ten aircraft.

At the same time, 15 IAR 81Cs were added to the dwindling strength of *Grupul 2 vânătoare* (*Escadrile 65* and *66*). In late February the inexperienced pilots of the new Bf 109G-*Grup* joined a few old hands, like the CO, *Lt c-dor av* Dan Vizanty, and *Of ech av* Ioan Milu, both of whom were top scoring aces, to fly combat missions.

On 21 February, C1AR CO *Gen esc av* Emanoil Ionescu met Col-Gen F F Ymachenko, CO of the Soviet 40th Army, to discuss the forthcoming joint offensive in the Zvolen (Zólyom/Altsohl) area. This was intended to breach the strong Hungarian-German defence. C1AR units were to provide air support for the attacking troops, and a record number of aircraft were prepared for action in what was to be the Rumanian flyers' last major combat operation of the war.

At 0530 hrs on 25 February, Bf 109Gs of *Grupul 9 vânătoare* took off from Lucenec in the pre-dawn darkness to join Savoia JRS-79 bombers from Oradea (Nagyvárad, Grosswardein) airfield. Miskolc-based Ju 88As rendezvoused with the formation at 0930 hrs, and initial Luftwaffe involvement was limited to a reconnaissance mission flown by a Bf 109 *Rotte*. From 1300 hrs, however, single-engined German fighters based at Piest'any (Pöstyén/Pistian) began to appear over the combat zone in larger numbers.

Grupul 2 vânătoare's Adj av Gheorghe Alexandru Grecu (left) and *Adj stag av* Pavel Vieru pose for an official photograph in late February 1945. Both have just been awarded the Red Banner Medal by the USSR for shooting down – on Soviet orders – a Rumanian Hs 129B-2 ground attack aircraft, piloted by *Adj av* Dumitru Marinescu, who was attempting to defect to German-held territory along with two comrades on 9 February 1945. The actual kill was attributed to Grecu. Ironically, Marinescu had flown with both men in *Gr 8 vân*. Grecu also wears the Aeronautical Virtue Cross with Swords above his left breast pocket. He was an eight-victory ace with three confirmed and one unconfirmed kills, all the confirmed victories being achieved while fighting on the Allied side. Vieru did not score. Behind them is the tail of IAR 80 'White 111'. Note the letter 'M' just above the middle '1' which indicates that the aircraft is a rare sub-version re-equipped with a 20 mm Mauser cannon. The suffix appeared only on aircraft modified by ASAM-Cotroceni. Also visible is the white rear fuselage ring and upper wingtips – a recognition feature for Allied aircraft flying in the operational area assigned to the VVS 5th *Vozdushnaya Armiya* (Air Force) to which the Rumanian *Corpul 1 Aerian* was subordinated at this time

ARR generals from Bucharest visit *Grupul 9 vânătoare* during the fighting in Transylvania in the autumn of 1944. Dressed in German-issue flying clothing, the pilots are, standing from left to right, *Adj maj av* Dumitru Goloiu (three victories), *Adj sef av* Constantin Ursache (11) and *Lt av* Ion Galea (12+). The four *Comandori aviator* at right are Dumitru Borcescu, Fenici, Ioan Govela and Alexandru Zaharescu. In the background is late production Bf 109G-6 'Red 2', fitted with an Erla canopy. Flying this aircraft (Wk-Nr. 166169), *Cpt rez av* Cantacuzino was shot down by a Luftwaffe Bf 109G over Slovakia on 25 February 1945. Note the lack of Rumanian tri-colour stripes, which were usually painted on the rudder. This photograph was taken at Cluj-Someseni airfield on 30 October 1944

Grupul 9 vânătoare's Cpt av Gheorghe Popescu-Ciocănel (right) and his favourite wingman, *Adj stag av* Traian Dârjan, enjoy a cigarette break between missions. On 15 April 1944, both pilots shot down an La-5 apiece in the Cârpiti-Popricani-Corbul triangle. Neither ace would survive the war. Popescu-Ciocănel was severely wounded during a dogfight with Mustangs on 26 July 1944, succumbing to his injuries on 12 August. By then he had achieved 18 victories. Dârjan was shot down by Hauptmann Helmut Lipfert, *Kommandeur* of I./JG 53, on 25 February 1945, by which time he was credited with 17 victories

In response, *Grupul 9 vânătoare* fighters, led by CO *Cpt rez av* Constantin Cantacuzino, took off from Lucenec at around 1400 hrs and soon spotted two Fw 190 *Schwarmen* attacking Soviet troops near Zvolen. The Rumanians dived on the numerically-superior enemy, and Cantacuzino, the ARR's leading ace, promptly shot down Fw 190F-8 'Yellow 7' (Wk-Nr. 584057) of 3./SG 2 near Vígl'as (Végles) village, killing pilot Gefreiter Hermann Heim. While watching his victim crash to ascertain the details needed to support his victory claim, Cantacuzino and his wingman, *Adj stag av* Traian Dârjan, failed to notice an approaching Luftwaffe Bf 109G *Rotte* led by 203-kill ace Hauptmann Helmut Lipfert, CO of I./JG 53. The Germans surprised the careless Rumanian aces and despatched both of them within seconds.

First to fall was Dârjan, who died in the cockpit of his 'Yellow 9' (Wk-Nr. 166248). *'Bâzu'* Cantacuzino was shot down seconds later, probably by another I./JG 53 pilot. Prince Cantacuzino was more fortunate than his wingman, for he was able to belly land his stricken Bf 109G-6 'Red 2' (Wk-Nr. 166169) behind the front, north-west of Detva, and just feet from the wreck of Dârjan's aircraft. Although his Fw 190F kill remained unconfirmed, it represented Cantacuzino's 69th, and last, victory.

Dârjan was the last ARR ace to be shot down and killed in aerial combat, his final tally standing at 12 enemy aircraft destroyed, representing at least 17 victories according to the ARR scoring system.

This eventful day was not over, however, for soon after Cantacuzino and his wingman were shot down, a Bf 109G *patrulă* took off to engage the increasing number of Luftwaffe aircraft operating in the area. Over the frontline, four ARR Messerschmitts were bounced from above by four identical Luftwaffe machines just west of Zv Slatina. In

Farewell to a fallen colleague. Comrades mourn *Adj stag rez av* Traian Dârjan, who was shot down and killed by Hauptmann Helmut Lipfert on 25 February 1945. His coffin, wrapped in the blue-yellow-red Rumanian flag and covered by pine branches, has been placed beneath the nose of a *Grupul 9 vânătoare* Bf 109G-6. By the time of his death, on his 176th combat sortie, Dârjan had scored at least 17 aerial victories

the ensuing dogfight two Rumanian Bf 109s were hit and both were forced to break off and head for home. One of the pilots, *Lt av* Horia Pop, later recalled seeing a chevron marking on the side of the German aircraft as it passed him, suggesting that its pilot was a *Staffelkapitän*. The only Luftwaffe pilot reported as claiming an aerial victory on that date and in that area, apart from Lipfert, was Oberleutnant Hans Kornatz of 1./JG 53. He claimed his 36th kill, over a Rumanian Bf 109G, near Altsohl. It is possible that his wingman, Fähnrich Schuhmacher, shot down the other Rumanian Bf 109, 'Yellow 2', flown by *Adj av* Laurentiu Manu.

Although badly mauled, the Rumanians managed to fight back through *Adj av* Constantin Nicoarā, who damaged a Bf 109K-4 from I./JG 53 so badly that it later crashed. Recent research has unearthed two more victory claims filed by *Gr 1 vân* pilots against Luftwaffe Bf 109s on this day, *Lt av* Constantin Fotescu and *Adj av* Ioan Nicola both reporting kills, although no matching losses can be found in Luftwaffe records.

After 25 February the Luftwaffe was seldom encountered over the Slovak front. It was considered by the OKW to be of secondary importance, and only one clash between fighters is recorded. This happened on 1 April when *Adj av* Constantin Nicoarā filed a claim for a Bf 109 which has only recently come to light in Rumanian archives. It represents the last official air-to-air combat victory claimed by the *vânātori* during World War 2.

From March 1945 most ARR fighter sorties took the form of escort missions, and these were assigned to Bf 109G units only. Low-level attacks were also flown on enemy positions and columns, although these were mostly undertaken by IAR 80/81s. Between 25 February and 24 March, the two Messerschmitt-equipped groups flew 105 missions (328 sorties) in 261 hours, which represented a creditable performance considering the reduced number of aircraft available.

On 26 March, *Grupul 1 vânātoare* sustained one of the few losses recorded for the period when a Bf 109G-2 *celulā*, comprising *Slt av* Aurelian Barbici and *Adj av* Virgil Angelescu disappeared while escorting bombers to Kremnica (Körmöcbánya, Kremnitz). But the two Rumanians were not shot down, for they had defected to the German side. 'Radio Danube', the German propaganda station, later announced that after a short flight at tree-top level, Bf 109Ga-2s 'Yellow 10' (IAR constr no 312) and 'Yellow 12' (constr no 304) had landed at Trentschin (Trencín, Trencsén) airfield.

According to German documentation, 'during interrogation, the two Rumanians expressed their willingness to fight against the Bolsheviks on the German side – in their view the only force capable of stopping the spread of Communism over their homeland'. While Barbici returned to Rumania after the war, claiming he had been shot down and imprisoned, the fate of Angelescu remains uncertain.

On 7 April, the two fighter *grupuri* moved from Lucenec to Tri Dvory (Badin) airfield, north of Zvolen, to support the forthcoming offensive of the Soviet 40th Army and the Rumanian 4th Army. The objective was Trencín, a strategically important town in western Slovakia. Although Luftwaffe fighters rarely appeared, German and

Locotenent aviator Mircea Teodorescu of *Grupul 1 vânătoare* leans against his Bf 109G-6, 'Red 1', in Slovakia in the spring of 1945. 'Shoto' Teodorescu's first clash with the enemy occurred during the very first USAAF attack against Rumania on 4 April 1944. Closing in on a Liberator, his IAR 80 was hit by defensive fire and he was wounded. Teodorescu was able to land safely at his home base at Rosiori de Vede, in southern Wallachia, but weak from loss of blood, he had to be helped from the cockpit by comrades, who placed him in an ambulance. Later, 21 bullet holes were counted in his IAR 80, 'White 388'. Released from hospital, Teodorescu was again hit in aerial combat on 5 May, but was not wounded this time, and he belly-landed his 'White 356' near Finta village. After Rumania's change of sides, he returned to the front in early 1945 to command a squadron within the re-equipped *Grupul 1 vânătoare*. Teodorescu finished the war with one confirmed Liberator kill, plus one probable, representing six victories under the ARR system

Hungarian flak remained efficient right to the end of the war. In fact, accurate flak defending a motorised column accounted for nine-victory ace *Lt av* Gheorghe Mociornitā of *Grupul 2 vânātoare*. His IAR 81C ('White 426') was shot down in flames over Vlcnov, north of Nemcice (Nyitranémeti/Niwnitz) during his 29th combat mission on 21 April.

Mociornitā's aircraft had arrived at the front from IAR's Brasov factory just three days earlier. Curiously, its engine cowling was still painted in the Axis yellow recognition colour, as indicated by the fragment which was recovered in the 1980s and exhibited in Bucharest's Military Museum. Mociornitā was the last ARR ace to fall in action.

On 4 May, Rumanian and Soviet fighters were involved in a peculiar incident. While returning to their base after a routine combat sortie, two *Grupul 1 vânātoare* pilots, *Of ech av* Ioan Milu, the ARR's third ranking ace, and *Lt av* Dumitru Baciu, an ace with ten victories, encountered several P-51Ds over northern Hungary. The Rumanians waggled their wings in greeting and the Americans responded. A few minutes later they met a formation of Il-2s, escorted by Yak-3s. Again, the Messerschmitt pilots waved, but the Soviets did not respond and continued in the opposite direction. Suddenly, the last two Yaks in the formation broke off and opened fire on the two Rumanians. The 43-year-old Milu, credited with destroying more than 24 Soviet aircraft, decided to dive away. He was caught and forced to crash land in Austrian territory at Straßhof an der Nordbahn.

The aggressive *'Take'* Baciu, however, accepted the challenge and began to dogfight with the Soviet pair. According to the (so far

Cpt av Dan Vizanty (left), CO of *Grupul 1 vânātoare*, chats with comrade and friend *Lt av* Dumitru Baciu in front of Vizanty's Bf 109G-6 'Red 1' in Slovakia in the spring of 1945. Note the different cut of the collars on the uniforms worn by each man. Both ex-IAR 81 pilots of *Grupul 6 vânātoare*, they had converted to the Bf 109G to fight against the Axis, and were credited with over 50 victories between them. It is believed that 'Take' Baciu was the last ARR pilot to claim an aerial kill in World War 2, which he achieved during a fight with a pair of Yak fighters – technically flown by the Rumanians' Soviet allies – who unexpectedly jumped him over Kromerziz, in the former German-run 'Protektorat' (today's Czech Republic), on 4 May 1945. The melee ended with both the Rumanian and his Russian attacker shooting each other down, Baciu crash-landing his bullet-riddled *Gustav* 'Red 3' (Wk-Nr. 166182) without injury

unconfirmed) memoirs of a former ARR pilot, Baciu shot down one of the Soviet fighters, but his aircraft was damaged and he force-landed near Kromeríz (Kremsler), 19 miles south-east of Olomouc (Olmütz). After climbing from his battered Bf 109G, one wing of which was torn off, Baciu counted over a dozen holes from machine gun and cannon fire. If the report is authentic, Baciu was the last ARR pilot to score an aerial victory, albeit one officially ignored.

Although Rumanian official documents mention crash landings by both Milu and Baciu, no further explanation is given. Baciu was killed shortly after the war by an armed thug while delivering mail in his Po-2 biplane, so he cannot tell his side of the story.

THE LAST OFFENSIVE

The final Allied offensive in the European theatre opened on 6 May, when Rumanian troops and aircraft were involved in Operation *Prague*. The fighters did their usual job of providing air cover and strafing enemy columns and positions. The last day of the war claimed the final victim among the *vânători*. The pilot of *Gr 2 vân* IAR 81C 'White 399', *Slt av* Remus Florin Vasilescu, was listed as missing in action in the Miklovice area after a strafing attack. On 9 May – VE-Day – ARR airmen were ordered to cease fire, but 11 surveillance missions were flown to monitor the Germans' surrender, with further sorties over the next few days. On 11 May, the CO of C1AR called for four volunteers to escort level and dive-bombers attacking units of the Russian anti-Communist Vlasov Army who refused to surrender and were still holed up around Prague. Four NCOs of *Grupul 9 vânătoare* reportedly volunteered for this final task, regarded as a matter of honour.

During the Czechoslovakian campaign, the C1AR's 88 fighters, which had been organised in three groups of two squadrons, flew 423 combat missions (1160 sorties) for a total of 975 hours. While no aerial victories were officially acknowledged, at least ten Rumanian fighters were lost, mainly to flak.

The ARR's fifth, and last, campaign of World War 2, fought between 24 August 1944 and 12 May 1945, had involved it in operations against its former Axis allies. At the start, 21 fighter squadrons had fielded a total of 210 serviceable aircraft – one-third below the level recorded in the

Lt av Ion Galea of *Grupul 9 vânătoare* poses with his personal *Gustav* in the spring of 1945. The aircraft's original German construction number, 166183, is just visible at the base of the rudder, and the previous owners' swastika marking is still displayed on the fin, although at this stage of war the Rumanians were fighting the Germans! Galea survived the war with at least 12 aerial victories. *Gen r av* Galea provided personal memories for this volume shortly before his death

Groundcrew prepare a factory-fresh IAR Brasov-built Bf 109Ga-6 for a combat sortie from Zvolen (Zólyom, Altsohl) airfield in early April 1945. The first Rumanian-assembled Bf 109Gs had started arriving at the front with the *Grupul 1 vânătoare* in late March, but saw little action as the Germans considered Slovakia to be a secondary theatre. This *Gustav* appears to be in pristine condition, in contrast to the patched and dirty appearance of the long-serving Bf 109Gs of *Grupul 9 vânătoare*, some of which had been captured from the Luftwaffe and hastily impressed into ARR service

spring of 1944, prior to the commencement of the USAAF attacks. It should, however, be noted that up to 20 August, combat losses of German-built aircraft were at least partially made good by the Luftwaffe. Approximately 60 to 80 ex-Luftwaffe fighters – Bf 109s and Bf 110s, as well as Fw 190s – could also be added to the total, together with an estimated 75 per cent of the 46 military aircraft built or assembled by IAR at Brasov up to May 1945.

From 6 September 1944 to the end of the war – the period of the so-called western front – the *vânātori* flew 701 combat missions (2367 sorties). Official Rumanian military statistics do not differentiate between claims filed by fighter pilots and flak gunners for enemy aircraft shot down. This was probably done on purpose in order to avoid highlighting the embarrassingly small number of enemy aircraft claimed by the ARR's fighter force. Some 101 enemy aircraft are officially noted as having been destroyed. The ARR's fighter losses are not separated from the overall figure, but at least 30 were destroyed by enemy action, with many others written off in accidents.

WAR ENDS AND UNCERTAINTY BEGINS

The end of the war provoked mixed feelings amongst the Rumanian fighter pilots. On VE-Day, *Lt av* Ion Dobran confided to his diary, 'After my final, 430th, combat sortie, I climb from the aircraft with regret. I am sad. I don't know why because in fact I should be happy'. On the final page of his wartime logbook *Lt av* Horia Pop posed a question which summed up the feelings of many combat veterans. 'The war is over, what now?'

Considering the events of the preceding eight months, with Rumania changing sides and the Soviets now installed in the country, the pilots' uncertainty was perfectly understandable. And an event which took place two months after the end of the war cannot have encouraged feelings of confidence for those involved.

On 11 and 12 July 1945, the first batch of approximately 40 Messerschmitts , accompanied by a similar number of IAR fighters, left Czechoslovakia and headed for Bucharest. Popesti-Leordeni airfield had been designated as the post-war base of *Flotila 1 vânătoare*, and when the first veteran fighter pilots, many with four years of war behind them, landed on the grassy field, they were amazed to find just a few cattle grazing peacefully. There was nobody there to meet them.

Reality was indeed harsh. Once the parades were over and the medals awarded, the strict terms of the peace treaty were imposed on Rumania. Its inventory of military aircraft was reduced to 150, with personnel cut to 10,000. By August 1947, the ARR had less than 75 fighters. Alongside reductions in equipment came the first substantial release of officers and NCOs from active duty. Many were even jailed for their participation in the anti-Soviet campaign. Sometimes they were accused of trumped up charges like 'unauthorised crossing of the USSR borders', and even simply 'being armed'.

All but a few veteran pilots, particularly those who had fought against the Soviets, and who remained loyal to the king, were discharged. They had to make way for a new generation of pilots whose origins were considered 'healthy', such as workers or peasants holding 'democratic' (that is pro-Communist) views. Soviet fighter

Lt av Ion Dobran – dubbed 'The Fakir' by his fellow pilots – poses with his Bf 109G-6 on a soaked Slovak airfield in the spring of 1945. One of the last surviving Rumanian Bf 109 aces from this era, *Gen ret av* Dobran recently published a personal diary containing vivid details of his wartime experiences, which included 74 aerial battles and 15 victories. In extensive interviews with the author, Dobran was able to give a rare insight into the daily life of the wartime *vânători*

A final group photo of *Grupul 9 vânătoare* pilots, taken after VE-Day at Miskolc airfield, in Hungary, on 31 July 1945. They are, standing from left to right, *Lt av* Stefan Octavian Ciutac (11 victories), *Lt av* Ion Dobran (15), *Adj av* Constantin Ursache (11), *Grup* CO *Cpt av* Emil Georgescu, (eight), *Lt av* Constantin Rosariu (33), *Cpt av* Ioan Micu (13), *Lt av* Mihai Lucaci (no score) and *Lt av* Mircea Senchea (nine). The two pilots in front of the group are *Lt av* Ion Galea (12+) and *Adj rez av* Ion Mălăcescu (21+). Note the long row of Bf 109Gs neatly lined up in the background

On the way back to Rumania on 31 July 1945, the *vânători* stopped at Miskolc, in Hungary, where this photograph was taken. *Lt av* Ion Galea took the opportunity to meet his fiancée, Klára (right), whom he later married, and her sister, Magda. Squadron CO *Cpt av* Teodor Greceanu perches casually on the stabiliser of Galea's battered late production Bf 109G-6 'Red 1'. The other pilots are *Lt av* Ion Dobran (behind the *Gustav*) and *Lt av* Mihai Lucaci (left). Note the IAR 80/81s in the background

Lt av Teodor Greceanu, dressed in a sheepskin Luftwaffe-issue pilot's jacket, poses beneath the spinner of his Bf 109G-6 in the spring of 1945. By this time he was credited with at least 24 victories, securing tenth place in the ARR's unofficial aces list. Later, as a *general de rezervă*, Greceanu claimed to have flown the Me 262 jet fighter during an impromptu demonstration to the Soviets, headed by Gen Selezniov, at Bratislava-Vajnory, in Slovakia, on 1 June 1945. But there is serious doubt about this claim, made to the author during a private interview the year before his death when Greceanu was already very ill. His wartime logbook does not record any such Me 262 flight

types (such as the Lavochkin La-9) gradually replaced the 'fascist' Bf 109G-6.

There is, though, one curious tailpiece to the story of Rumania's fighter arm in World War 2 which remains to be told. On 1 June 1945, several Rumanian pilots are reported to have taken part in a big airshow organised by the Soviets at Vajnory (Pozsonyszöllös) airfield, near Bratislava (Pozsony or Preßburg), now the capital of Slovakia, to demonstrate the capabilities of German technology in comparison with the latest Soviet and US types.

Among the Rumanians present was *Cpt av* Teodor Greceanu, the tenth ranking ARR ace with 24+ victories. He was flying his personal fighter, 'Red 316', which was also the first Bf 109Ga-6 assembled by IAR-Brasov. During an interview given to the author shortly before his death, Greceanu claimed that he had been given a unique chance to fly an Me 262 jet fighter which had been taken to Bratislava for evaluation. However, his log book records that he made only a one-hour demonstration flight in his Bf 109Ga-6 on that day, so his claim, made late in his life, must be considered highly doubtful.

Whatever the real truth behind this episode, the fact remains that by the late 1940s, the story of one of the most powerful fighter arms of Eastern Europe, and its celebrated pilots, had reached an inglorious conclusion. Rumania would remain a Soviet satellite for the next 40 years, but the deeds of its valiant *vânători* would certainly not be forgotten.

LEADING ACES

Among the many Rumanian fighter pilots whose deeds during World War 2 are celebrated, the careers of the leading four aces are selected here for more detailed study.

Constantin Cantacuzino

Born in Bucharest on 1 November 1905 to a noble and wealthy family, Prince Cantacuzino – known to his mother as *'Bâzu'*, a nickname which stayed with him for the rest of his life – showed great aptitude for many sports from an early age, winning several national and international trophies. It was natural that he should be attracted to aviation, and at the age of 27, Cantacuzino enrolled in a private flying school at Bucharest-Băneasa run by his relative, Ioana Cantacuzino. Showing outstanding talent, he received his 'tourism' pilot's licence, first class (basic level) after only two weeks of tuition! The second-class licence was achieved in August 1933, and two years later Prince Cantacuzino gained his multi-engine transport pilot's licence, joining Rumania's national airline, LARES.

The wealthy Cantacuzino bought his first private aircraft, a US-made Fleet F-10D biplane, that same year. He was to own others, including various Caudron, Fleet, ICAR and Bücker types, gaining the experience to perfect his skills undertaking long-range flights and performing aerobatics. Indeed, he became so proficient at the latter that he won Rumania's national aerobatics championship in 1939. *'Bâzu'* was undoubtedly the most prominent Rumanian flyer of the 1930s.

Prior to the war against the Soviets, Cantacuzino had been called up for duty as a 1st Lieutenant in the reserve, although his job with LARES would have exempted him from military service. He was assigned to one of the elite ARR fighter units, *Escadrila 53 vânătoare*, which he joined on 5 July 1941 after the war had started. The unit was equipped with Hurricanes, and Cantacuzino claimed his first kill less than a week after his initial combat sortie.

On 11 July, he was credited with downing a Soviet DB-3 bomber

Cpt rez av Constantin Cantacuzino became the top scoring Rumanian fighter pilot of World War 2. Before joining the ARR, he was a well-known, and highly skilled, flyer, winning the Rumanian aerobatics championship in July 1939. Cantacuzino is pictured in front of his biplane, a US-made Fleet F-10D, registered YR-ABY, at Le Bourget airport, Paris, in 1938

Two top surviving ARR aces, *Cpt rez av* Constantin Cantacuzino (centre, right) and *Cpt av* Dan Vizanty, give an interview to journalists beneath a Stuka at Lucenec airfield, in Slovakia, in April 1945. Both wear the distinctive *Mihai Viteazul* Order, their German Iron Crosses having long since disappeared. By this time these two aces were credited with at least 112 ARR aerial victories between them

near Izmail. Two days later he claimed two more bombers, but only one was confirmed. During the action Cantacuzino's Hurricane was hit by the bombers' defensive fire, forcing him to make an emergency landing at Tulcea, near his crashed victim. After a further two days, he downed another pair of DB-3 bombers, both of which were confirmed. His final kill in the Bessarabian campaign was claimed on 1 August, but remained unconfirmed. Having exculsively shot down bombers – the sole Rumanian pilot to do so – Cantacuzino was credited with a total of 12 victories under the ARR scoring system, and was third in the unofficial list of aces in 1941.

At the end of the ARR's first campaign, Cantacuzino returned to LARES, where he was promoted to chief pilot. Performing both domestic and international passenger flights, he had had also logged 45 transport sorties to the front by the end of 1942. During this time he participated in a ten-day Bf 109E conversion course, and took the opportunity to fly a captured Soviet MiG-3 fighter which had been landed at Melitopol airfield in December 1941 by a defecting Ukrainian pilot.

By May 1943 Cantacuzino's repeated requests to return to combat had resulted in his arrival at Tiraspol, where selected Rumanian fighter pilots were converting onto the Bf 109G. After carefully studying the cockpit and instrument panel, he is reported to have climbed in and taken off without further ado. With the new *Gustav*, he was on his way to the front the next day, having been assigned to *Grupul 7 vânătoare*. There, he replaced *Lt rez av* Polizu, who had achieved the most victories in the 1941 campaign, but had been killed in action on 6 May.

Cantacuzino's first success with the new aircraft (Bf 109G-4 'White 4' Wk-Nr. 19546) was logged on 29 June 1943 when he downed a pair of Soviet Spitfires near Alexandrovka. During the dogfight with the British-built fighters, flown by élite Soviet pilots, his aircraft was repeatedly hit in the engine and wings, forcing Cantacuzino to crash-land in friendly territory. During his next engagement with the enemy, on 18 July, *'Bâzu'* claimed two LaGG-3s and one Il-2 in the Kuybishev-Dmitrievka area, although only one of the fighter kills was confirmed due to a lack of witnesses.

Cpt rez av Cantacuzino was now engaged in an unofficial contest with the other leading ace, *Cpt av* Serbănescu. By the end of August 1943, when he was recalled to Rumania, Cantacuzino had shot down 27 enemy aircraft (which represented 28 victories under the ARR system) during his second spell on the eastern front. All bar one were fighters and ground-attack aircraft, the exception being a reconnaissance Pe-2 shot down over Kuteilnikovo on 27 July. Adding his 1943 score to that achieved in 1941 made Cantacuzino the top-scoring Rumanian pilot with 36 aerial victories (25 confirmed and 11 probables).

One of the ace's many outstanding performances was a series of 28 night interceptions of Soviet intruders made in June-July 1943. Not only were these without any formal training, but they were undertaken with a standard Bf 109G operating from an airfield illuminated only by a few fuel drums for take-off and landing.

Although Cantacuzino did not claim any victories during this time, his achievement remained unique in the ARR.

The air war changed in April 1944 with the appearance over Rumania of the USAAF, and in early April Cantacuzino was assigned to *Escadrila 57 vânătoare* of *Grupul 7 vânătoare*, tasked with defending the capital. His first USAAF kill came on 15 April when he shot down a B-24D over Bucharest. Yet despite the three victories credited to him following the destruction of the four-engined Liberator, Cantacuzino was only second in the aces' list, for Serbănescu had scored heavily during the of winter of 1943-44 when the former was confined to hospital with scarlet-fever.

With the frontline rapidly approaching Rumania's north-eastern borders, *Gr 7 vân* was re-deployed to Moldavia in late April to face an increasingly aggressive enemy. Just days after relocation to Gherăesti-Bacău, Cantacuzino reported his first victory over a Yak in the Iasi (Yassy) region on 28 April. Five days later, he scored a triple against Soviet fighters, although he was officially credited with a pair of Airacobras. On 5 May came another Airacobra, followed by a Yak-7 the next day. The ace also claimed a pair of Yak-9s during the course of the month, but neither was confirmed.

In June 1944 Cantacuzino got another opportunity to fight USAAF aircraft flying shuttle missions to and from the USSR. On the 6th, he was at last able to frame a P-51 (the fighter he most admired) in the gunsight of his *Gustav*. Following an intense dogfight, the Mustang crash-landed at Vārdita-Tighina, its pilot, Lt John D Mumford of the 325th FG, escaping towards Soviet lines. Later in the month Cantacuzino shot down two Liberators, the second being shared with his wingman, *Adj rez av* Constantin Lungulescu. After destroying a Yak-9 on 28 June, he got another chance to 'bag' a P-51. However, the kill, claimed on 15 July, remained unconfirmed. Following two more Soviet fighters downed on 20 and 23 July, '*Bâzu*' scored a double against P-38Js of the 82nd FG on 4 August.

Serbănescu's unfortunate death gave Cantacuzino the opportunity to move ahead. Increasing air activity at the front resulting from the powerful Soviet offensive of 20 August in the Yassy-Kishinev sector offered further scoring chances. He took full advantage and shot down a Yak fighter on the opening day of the offensive, adding three more the next day.

The Rumanian *coup d'état* of 23 August 1944 changed the political and military situation dramatically, and Cantacuzino was given a delicate diplomatic mission to fulfil when he was asked to contact the Allies as soon as possible, and convey to them Rumanian peace terms. '*Bâzu*' took the highly unusual step of flying to Italy in a Bf 109G-6Y, formerly 'Red 31' (Wk-Nr. 166133), taking with

Watched by *Cpt rez av* Constantin Cantacuzino, *Adj stag av* Emil Bālan (ten victories prior to being killed in action on 26 July 1944) of *Escadrila 57 vânătoare, Grupul 9 vânătoare*, paints another victory stripe on the fin of the former's Bf 109G-4. The white stripes, each topped by a small red star, represent victories achieved over Soviet aircraft. The 40th stripe denotes a P-39 Airacobra shot down by Cantacuzino near Iasi (Jassy), capital of Moldavia, on 3 May 1944. As a reserve officer, Cantacuzino was not always in a combat unit, and the P-39 was his first kill after returning to the front following an absence of almost a year. '*Bâzu*' Cantacuzino would down a Yak-9 soon after this photo was taken

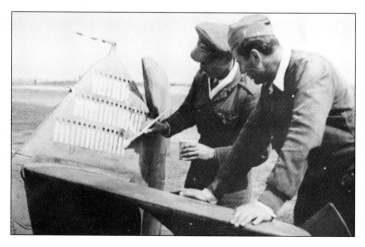

him, hidden in the fuselage, the highest-ranking American PoW in Rumania, Lt Col James Gunn III. To the amazement of the Americans, the two airmen landed at Foggia, Italy, on 27 August. Cantacuzino returned the next day, this time at the controls of a Mustang, despite having had no instruction on how to fly the aircraft. He flew back to Italy a couple of days later, returning with yet another Mustang.

Cantacuzino joined the new *Grupul 7/9 vânătoare* in October 1944 as the frontline advanced into Hungary, but this time to fight the Axis. He was appointed *Grup* CO following the death of *Cpt av* Lucian Toma. During the last months of 1944, the decimated Luftwaffe was seldom present in what was regarded as a secondary area of the eastern front, and Cantacuzino was not able to increase his score. However, he had claimed eight victories on 25 and 26 August against four He 111Hs of I./KG 4 that were attempting to attack Bucharest, these successes placing him top of the ARR victory list.

The chance to fight Luftwaffe fighters finally came on 25 February 1945. Cantacuzino and his wingman, *Adj stag av* Dârjan, were on a free-hunt when they sighted a formation of Fw 190s raiding Allied troops near Detva, Slovakia. Having promptly accounted for an Fw 190F of 3./SG 2, both Rumanian pilots were then bounced by a Luftwaffe Bf 109G *Rotte* that had been lurking above them. Dârjan was mortally wounded, while Cantacuzino belly-landed behind the frontline. His last encounter with the enemy brought his 69th, and final, aerial victory, although it was not confirmed due to the death of his only witness.

Constantin Cantacuzino ended his career as a fighter pilot at the age of 40, having flown 608 combat sorties and fought in 210 aerial battles. He also held the distinction of being an ace against all three major air forces that the Rumanians had fought, namely the VVS, the USAAF and the Luftwaffe. On 11 November 1946 he received his second Order of *'Mihai Viteazul'* with Spades, Third Class, the first having been conferred on him in August 1943.

Post-war, Cantacuzino returned to LARES – now renamed TARS – to resume his career as a commercial pilot, although the growing Soviet influence on Rumania, and the persecution faced by most Rumanian airmen from the new pro-Communist Rumanian régime, prompted Cantacuzino to defect while he had the chance. During a routine flight to Milan on 13 January 1948, he decided not to return to his homeland. He moved to France and then Spain, where he died on 26 May 1958 aged just 53. The cause of his death remains uncertain. The most famous Rumanian civil and military pilot, and the country's top scoring ace, Prince Constantin Cantacuzino is buried in Madrid.

Rumania's top scoring ace *Cpt rez av* Constantin Cantacuzino prepares to take off in his 'trophy' Mustang from Popesti-Leordeni airfield, near Bucharest, in late August 1944. He had been given *Sweet Clara* a couple of days earlier at Foggia, in Italy, in place of his Bf 109G-6Y 'Red 31 (Wk-Nr. 166133), which he had used to transport the highest-ranking captive USAAF airman in Rumania, Lt Col James A Gunn III, to Italy as part of a secret diplomatic mission. Soon after their surprise arrival at Gunn's Italian base, Cantacuzino's *Gustav* was damaged on take-off by an American pilot who wanted to try it out. According to wartime sources, Cantacuzino simply traded the Messerschmitt for the Mustang, a type he had been eager to fly since meeting it in combat. 'His' machine was war-weary P-51B-15 43-24857, which had previously been flown by five-kill ace Maj Robert M Barkey of the 319th/325th FG. Ironically, Barkey claimed at least one Rumanian Bf 109G kill while flying this aircraft

Alexandru Serbãnescu

Born in Colonesti-Vlaici, Olt County, on 17 May 1912, Alexandru Serbãnescu graduated from the school for infantry officers at Sibiu as a *Sublocotenent* in 1933 and joined a mountain troop unit at Brasov. In early 1939, he entered the school for aerial observers and received his wings later that same year. Serbãnescu enrolled at pilots' school in 1940 when already 28, and received his combat pilots' brevet on 31 October. Posted to fighters, he flew PZL P.11s, IAR 80s and then Bf 109Es.

In April 1942, *Locotenent aviator* Serbãnescu was transferred to *Grupul 7 vânãtoare*, arriving in the combat area on 2 September with *Escadrila 57 vânãtoare*. His first combat missions took place over Stalingrad, and he was soon placed in temporary command after the squadron CO was shot down and killed on 12 September. The breakthrough for Serbãnescu came on 17 September when he scored his first kill, a Yak-1 north-east of Stalingrad. Eight days later he claimed another victory over an I-153 north-west of Kotluban, but the claim was not confirmed. By 17 November he had logged the group's highest number of combat sorties.

Having some experience of ground combat, Serbãnescu organised his men to repulse the Soviet attack on Karpovka airfield on 22 November 1942. Under his leadership, a handful of airmen took off in the squadron's airworthy *Emils* before dawn, each carrying a member of the squadron's groundcrew. On 20 January 1943, Serbãnescu and his wingman, *Adj stag rez av* Tiberiu Vinca, flew a free hunt mission over the Bataisk-Manitschkaya area. Over Kudinov, they clashed with several Soviet Hurricanes, and each Rumanian claimed a victory.

Serbãnescu's exploits were recognised by his promotion to captain on 6 March 1943. Soon afterwards, 30 pilots were selected to form an experimental joint German-Rumanian fighter unit within *Jagdgeschwader 3 'Udet'*, which became known as *Deutsch-Königlich Rumänischen Jagdverband*. Serbãnescu was appointed CO of *Escadrila 57 vânãtoare*, one of three ARR squadrons assigned to the mixed unit. The Rumanians arrived at Pavlograd airfield, southern Ukraine, in early March, and received brand new Bf 109Gs. By the end of the

This wartime Rumanian propaganda photograph of Alexandru Serbãnescu was captioned 'The Eagle of Wallachia and The Green Pine of the Carpathian Mountains'. Serbãnescu was the second ranking ARR ace with 55 aerial victories, and is universally respected by surviving Rumanian airmen, who consider him to be the ultimate hero of the wartime ARR. With his death in action, fighting an enemy both numerically and technically superior, he avoided being 'tainted' by involvement in the fighting against Rumania's former Axis partners. On the anniversary of his death, surviving fighter pilots have gathered at his grave at Ghencea Military Cemetery in Bucharest – a custom observed even during Communist rule – to remember Serbãnescu. Sadly, the numbers of veteran *vânãtori* are dwindling every year

The recently-promoted *Cpt av* Alexandru Serbãnescu, CO of *Grupul 7 vânãtoare*, is briefed by subordinate *Adj av* Nicolae Iolu (five victories) before flying a sortie over Stalingrad in early March 1943. By that time only three serviceable Bf 109Es and one He 111H remained available, and these were assembled in a make-shift mixed unit called *Grupul mixt Comandor aviator Iosifescu*, named after its CO, Nicolae Iosifescu. The sole victory symbol on this particular *Emil* is dated 27 June 1941, denoting a Soviet fighter destroyed on the ground at Bulgãrica airfield

month the first combat missions had been flown over the front in the face of a strong Soviet presence.

It was at this time that Serbănescu began to excel as a leader, and to build up a significant combat score. He started on 5 April, claiming a Yak-7 south of Izyum. Three days later, a LaGG-5 shot down northwest of the same locality elevated Serbănescu to ace status. By the end of the month he was credited with two more kills, followed by a probable in May. Having scored eight aerial victories during the course of 200+ combat missions, Serbănescu had placed himself firmly in the top echelon of ARR *vânători*.

Following the experimental fighter unit's disbandment on 1 June 1943, Serbănescu and his squadron continued to fight within *Corpul 1 Aerian Român* in the area between the rivers Donets and Mius. He also continued to pile up victory after victory, and in June claimed three more VVS fighters, including a Spitfire, downed on the 26th near Tshaltye.

On 5 July, Serbănescu was awarded the Order of *Virtutea Aeronautică*, Cavalier's Cross Class. His luck deserted him four days later, however, when he was wounded in the face by ground fire while strafing an enemy troop column. His eyes covered in blood, and barely able to see, Serbănescu managed to bring his Bf 109G-4 (Wk-Nr. 14865) home, but he crashed on landing and the aircraft was 80 per cent damaged. Barely recovered from his injury, the ace was wounded again on 20 August, leaving him with a permanent facial scar.

August 1943 was Serbănescu's most successful month, with ten confirmed and two unconfirmed victories – all but three of his victims were tough Il-2s. In fact, these victories made him the top Rumanian *Shturmovik* killer with ten confirmed and four probables. Serbănescu was selected as one of the five top ARR fighter pilots to receive the prestigious Order of *Mihai Viteazul*, Third Class, on 30 August 1943, by which time he had 15 confirmed and four unconfirmed aerial victories – all fighters or ground attack aircraft – to his credit. Just days earlier the Germans had also rewarded him for his efforts in the common struggle against the Soviets by presenting him with the Iron Cross, First Class.

Cpt av Alexandru Serbănescu is congratulated on his latest aerial victory in the late summer of 1943 at Mariupol airfield. These men are, from left to right, an unknown mechanic, *Cpt av* Lucian Toma (13+ victories by the time he was killed in action on 25 September 1944), *Adj rez av* Constantin Lungulescu (24+ victories by the time he was killed in action on 24 June 1944), Serbănescu (55 victories by the time he was killed in action on 18 August 1944), an unidentified officer-pilot and technician officer *Lt mec* Marin Bâscă. Behind them is Serbănescu's all dark green Bf 109G-2/R6 Wk-Nr. 13755, which is equipped with a pair of underwing gondolas housing 20 mm cannon. Although this additional armament cut the fighter's top speed by 19 mph, experienced pilots like Serbănescu and Milu preferred the added 'punch' the guns gave the Bf 109G in combat

Three weeks' leave meant that Serbănescu could only score once in September, and the Yak-1 he claimed while escorting Rumanian Ju 87Ds was listed as a probable. On the first day of October he claimed his very first multi-engined aircraft, a lend-lease Boston bomber, east of Biriutski Island. Two days later, he downed another Yak fighter, followed by a Yak-9 on 5 October. Another four kills were claimed that month, including a double on the 28th over a pair of Yaks in the Akimovka area. There were to be no more victories that year, but it was not the end of the excitement.

On 10 October, Serbănescu was reported to have force-landed his blazing aircraft in no-man's land after a fierce dogfight with enemy fighters. He was rescued by soldiers of the 4th Mountain Division, and his aircraft – the first Bf 109G-6 delivered to the Rumanians, 'Yellow 44' (Wk-Nr. 15854) – was recovered later.

By the end of 1943, Serbănescu, assigned to *Grupul 9 vânătoare*, had flown 368 combat sorties, fought 126 aerial battles and was credited with 27 confirmed victories and six probables.

There was more action in 1944, as the Axis tried to hold the advancing Soviets. In January, Serbănescu was credited with a confirmed and a probable kill. The former was gained while single-handedly fighting 11 Yak fighters over his base, Lepetikha airfield, on the 14th. During February and March, he was able to add only one more victory to his score in each month, but he achieved them as CO of *Grupul 9 vânătoare*, having been given command on 9 February.

Soviet pressure increased in April as the Red Army crossed Rumania's north-eastern borders, and Serbănescu shot down two Yaks north of Iasi. It was at this time that he passed the score of his main rival Constantin Cantacuzino, who was at that time credited with 39 victories under the ARR scoring system, although in terms of the actual number of aircraft shot down Serbănescu was ahead. On 20 April, he logged his 500th combat sortie.

May was the busiest month for the ARR, and during the last ten days Serbănescu was credited with a *Shturmovik* and five enemy fighters – all lend-lease P-39s – including a double scored on the 25th.

Air minister *General de escadră aviator* Gheorghe Jienescu decorates *Cpt av* Alexandru Serbănescu during a ceremony held before *Grupul 9 vânătoare*. Behind the recipient are *Cpt rez av* Constantin Cantacuzino and *Adj rez av* Constantin Lungulescu (24 victories), while on Serbănescu's left, several *Grup* pilots can also be recognised – *Lt rez av* Ioan Simionescu (five victories) and *Of ech cl III av* Ioan Milu (52). Note the difference between the smartly-dressed career officer Serbănescu and the rather sloppy-looking Cantacuzino, a reserve pilot of noble origin who regarded his participation in the war as being more of a sport than a strict military duty. It is said that the two men, who competed for top position in the aces' list, did not get along well, and were seldom photographed together

Cpt av Alexandru Serbănescu (right) and *Of ech cl III av* Ioan Milu share a joke in front of a *Grupul 9 vânătoare Gustav* at Tecuci airfield in June 1944. Both wear the Iron Cross First Class and *Frontflugspange* in Gold. Additionally, Milu's tunic is decorated with the *Mihai Viteazul* Order and the ribbon of the Iron Cross, Second Class

With these victories he became the joint top Rumanian Airacobra killer, a distinction he shared with *Adj av* Cristea Chirvăsută, the sixth ranking ARR ace with 31 victories.

There was a lull in the fighting on the eastern front during June and July, by which time a new enemy had appeared in Rumanian skies – the USAAF. The first real chance for Serbănescu to clash with the American intruders came on 11 June when he shot down a B-17 Flying Fortress. The next American aircraft that he claimed to have destroyed was a P-38

A Mountain Troop officer (extreme right) visits his former comrade *Cpt av* Alexandru Serbănescu (second from left) at Tecuci airfield in June 1944. Standing between them are the following *Grupul 9 vânătoare* pilots, from left to right, *Lt av* Hariton 'Tony' Dusescu (12 victories), possibly *Adj sef av* Andrei Rădulescu (18), *Lt av* Mircea Senchea (nine), *Of ech cl III av* Ioan Milu (52), *Lt av* Ion Dobran (15) and an unknown airman

Lightning on 22 July, although this remains unconfirmed. On the last day of the month Serbănescu shot down a P-51, with another following on 4 August. But the ranking Rumanian ace could not know that this P-51D of the 52nd FG, which crashed close to Independenta railway station, was to be his 52nd, and final, victim.

On 18 August 1944, the outnumbered and outgunned Rumanians were practically shot out of the sky by scores of P-51s from the 31st FG. The heaviest blow was the loss of the commander of *Grupul 9 vânătoare Deßloch-Serbănescu*, Cpt av Serbănescu himself. Flying an aircraft with a faulty radio, he was bounced at high altitude by Mustangs. Unable to hear his wingman's warning, Serbănescu's stricken Bf 109G-6 crashed near Brasov, in the Rusavăt Valley.

At the time of his death, the 32-year-old Alexandru Serbănescu was the top-scoring ARR fighter ace in terms of the number of aircraft destroyed, having been credited with 47 confirmed victories and eight probables. In his two-year career as a fighter pilot, he had flown 590 combat sorties and fought in 235 aerial battles. Serbănescu was nominated for the Order of *Mihai Viteazul*, Second Class, a distinction not accorded to any active ARR pilot. But Rumania changed sides only five days after his death, and the decoration was not awarded.

Killed fighting an enemy that enjoyed both numerical and technical supremacy, and not 'tainted' by any involvement in the war against the Axis, Serbănescu soon became a legend among his compatriots. After 23 August 1944, it was no longer 'politically correct' to mention his name, but Serbănescu was celebrated once again after the fall of communism in December 1989. Today, a boulevard in Bucharest has been named after Alexandru Serbănescu – a unique tribute to a wartime Rumanian fighter pilot.

Ioan Milu

Born in 1902 in Brasov, Ioan Milu was drawn to aviation at an early age. Barely 18, he was an apt pupil at the local flying school, and flew World War 1 era biplanes. He joined the air force as a *Sergent aviator*

79

in 1922, and 12 years later decided to transfer to the ARR's elite fighter force. Because of his qualifications, he was assigned to the top fighter unit, *Flotila 1 vânătoare*, which came into being on 1 January 1937. Milu flew the gull-winged Polish PZL P.11, which was then the mainstay of the ARR's fighter arm. During the modernisation programme, he was involved in the introduction of new fighter types.

On the first day of the war against the Soviet Union, Milu was a member of the Bf 109E-equipped *Escadrila 56 vânătoare*, based at Râmnicul Sărat, in southern Moldavia. He flew escort missions and air interdiction sorties, which occasionally involved air combat as well as ground strafing. *Adj sef av* Ioan Milu ended the ARR's first campaign in 1941 credited with three enemy aircraft shot down.

Milu did not fight over Stalingrad, instead flying coastal patrol and home-defence missions. He took advantage of this comparatively uneventful period to pass the rigorous examination necessary for an NCO to advance to the rarely-assigned rank of warrant officer third class.

Following the ARR's reorganisation and re-equipment with the latest German types in the spring of 1943, selected *Grupul 7 vânătoare* pilots, including Milu, were temporarily assigned to III./JG 3, the famous *'Udet' Jagdgeschwader*. Soon after the unit's arrival at Pavlograd, Ioan Milu opened his scoring on 10 April 1943 with an aircraft destroyed on the ground at Starobielsk airfield. It was not, however, confirmed under the strict German rules. But his second claim, filed a few days later – a Pe-2, which crashed in flames south-west of Kramatorskaya – was. Another confirmed aerial victory followed two weeks later when he shot down an Il-2 east of Krasniy Liman. It was Milu's fifth official aerial victory, and it made him an ace – at 41, Rumania's oldest.

Milu's best day with the *'Udet' Geschwader* came on 6 May when, after a bombing run, he single-handedly shot down three LaGG-3s in two separate battles involving a total of ten Soviet fighters. By the time the experimental unit was disbanded on 1 June 1943, Ioan Milu was credited with four aircraft confirmed destroyed and three unconfirmed.

After scoring his last aerial victory as a member of JG 3 – a MiG-3 shot down without witnesses on 16 May – Milu enjoyed a period of comparative calm. But August 1943 was to be the most successful month of his fighter career, although it almost ended in tragedy. He opened his scoring on the 4th by downing his tenth victim – an unidentified VVS fighter – while escorting a Luftwaffe reconnaissance aircraft. Three days later, Milu 'bagged' two Il-2s in five minutes, and added a further Soviet machine to his score on the 13th. But the highlight of his career came on 16 August, when he shot down five enemy aircraft to establish a record unbeaten by any other Rumanian fighter pilot.

On that day, 22 enemy aircraft were confirmed as being destroyed by ARR fighters, with another five unconfirmed, during 15 aerial battles. Milu's tally was three Il-2s and two 'B-8s' (possibly A-20 Boston bombers). There was more success two days later, when he downed a VVS aircraft, followed by a fighter 24 hours later. In fact,

A fine portrait of the third ranking Rumanian ace, *Of ech cl III av* Ioan Milu, enjoying a cigarette with German pilots in the summer of 1944. Then aged 42, Milu was the oldest Rumanian fighter pilot in the frontline. He is wearing the *Mihai Viteazul* Order, Third Class, a *Frontflugspange* in Gold and Iron Cross, First Class, along with his Rumanian pilot's badge. On the sleeve of his uniform is the ARR airman's cloth patch alongside the stripe denoting his rank. Note the rather mediocre quality of the uniform's fabric

Ioan Milu poses in the cockpit of his Bf 109G-6, which the ARR had just received from the Luftwaffe. Small in stature, but energetic and aggressive, he emerged as the third ranking ARR ace, scoring 52 victories during the course of 500+ combat sorties that spanned the entire war. Note that the first letter of the factory *Stammkennzeichen* (call sign) is just visible behind the cockpit canopy

the latter engagement almost ended the ace's career.

At 1400 hrs, Milu and his wingman, *Adj av* Vasile Firu, together with another pair of Bf 109Gs, joined Hs 129s in the Dubrovka sector. Soon after they crossed the frontline, four Yaks jumped them from higher altitude. In the ensuing dogfights, Milu managed to shoot down one of the attackers, but eight LaGGs then joined the battle. The Rumanians were outnumbered three to one, and when the two ARR elements became separated, Milu and Firu were left to face the newcomers alone. Firu was overwhelmed by the LaGGs, which scored several hits on his Messerschmitt. Seeing his wingman's desperate situation, Milu rushed to his aid and, with his tail now unprotected, allowed one of the Soviet pilots to close in. Turning his head, the Rumanian ace could see a LaGG fighter with a distinctive white cowling and a large flower painted on its fuselage. It was directly behind him, firing away. He barely escaped his attacker – probably a VVS ace – and was eventually able to belly land his stricken fighter in friendly territory.

Milu returned to Kramatorskaya at dusk, by which time he was posted as missing in action. He arrived just in time to be decorated by Luftwaffe officers with the coveted Iron Cross, First Class, for outstanding achievements towards the Axis cause.

Ioan Milu returned to the front in early autumn 1943, and on 23 October sent a Yak fighter down into the Sea of Azov. Two days later, he scored what was to be his final victory of the year. At the time his victory tally exceeded 20, placing the 'old hand' in the top echelon of Rumanian aces.

At the end of October *Grupul 7 vânătoare* was recalled to Rumania, being replaced by its sister group, *Grupul 9 vânătoare*, and Milu did not fire his guns in anger again until well into 1944.

His first victim of the year, according to contemporary documents, was a 'new type' of Soviet bomber, later identified as a twin-engined lend-lease Douglas Boston, which he sent crashing to the ground near Hârlău on 15 April. The second, reportedly an 'Il-7' fighter downed between Iasi and Tg Frumos, followed two days later. The ace claimed a Yak-7, north of Moldavia's capital Iasi, on 28 April, and on 24 May destroyed a DB-3 north-east of Buhăesti-Roman railway station for his 30th kill. Milu ended the month by shooting down a P-39, which crashed near Tg Sculeni on 30 May.

His first victorious encounter with the USAAF took place on 11 June 1944, when a formation of B-17s, escorted by P-51s, returned from Soviet bases via Rumanian airspace. Thirteen Bf 109Gs scrambled to intercept the Americans at 23,000 ft over Focsani, and in the ensuing melee, Milu shot down one of the five Flying Fortresses credited that day to *Grupul 9 vânătoare*. His next victim, whilst flying with his ace wingman Traian Dârjan, was a Soviet Pe-2 reconnaissance aircraft caught over southern Bessarabia on 20 June. It crashed in Soviet-held territory east of Odessa without independent witness, so was not confirmed by the ARR.

In July, the USAAF intensified its raids on Rumania, and Milu scored another Flying Fortress kill in the middle of the month. On the 31st he had his first encounter with the P-38 Lightning, from which he emerged victorious. The dogfight developed above the Ploiesti oilfields, and Milu sent his victim crashing to earth at Valea Călugărească to add another two victories to his score.

Ofiser de echipaj clasa a III-a aviator **Ioan Milu (left) describes the engagement he has just fought against USAAF fighters in July 1944. Listening, from left to right, are an unidentified Army 2nd Lieutenant, the CO of** *Corpul 1 Aerian Român* **Gen esc av Emanoil 'Pipitzu' Ionescu (Knight of the Iron Cross), air minister** *Gen esc av* **Gheorghe Jienescu (partially obscured) and** *Cpt rez av* **Constantin Cantacuzino**

In an undated ARR document, which was probably prepared at the end of July 1944, Ioan Milu is credited with 430 combat sorties and a confirmed total of 30 enemy aircraft shot down or destroyed on the ground during the course of 150+ combats. He also set a T-34 tank on fire.

Ioan Milu was not to know that his next encounter with USAAF fighters was also to be his last. On 8 August, an 18-strong formation of Rumanian Bf 109Gs took off from Buzău airfield and joined a similar number of Luftwaffe fighters from Mizil. Led by Alexandru Serbănescu, the Rumanian force clashed with Eighth Air Force B-17s, escorted by a large number of P-51s, as they returned to England, via Italy, from the USSR. In his second pass on the enemy 'box', Milu scored fatal hits on a P-51, which crashed near Tăndărei.

Having expended all his ammunition on his 52nd kill, the ace was then jumped by a pair of Mustangs from above and his Bf 109G set on fire. Milu had to bale out, but the air stream pinned him to the fuselage of his crippled aircraft as it hurtled towards the ground at over 600 mph. It was only after the Messerschmitt started to break up, and then made a sudden roll, that Milu was finally freed. Opening his parachute just in time, he still hit the ground fairly hard, sustaining further injuries. Rumania's oldest fighter ace was now definitely out of action, confined to a hospital bed for the next two months.

By the time Milu recovered, his country's political and military situation had changed dramatically. He resumed flying as an instructor just as *Grupul 1 vânătoare* re-equipped with the Bf 109G, and in mid-February he deployed with the group to southern Slovakia. However, there was little Axis activity on what was a secondary front, thus Milu could not add to his score.

On 16 December 1946, Milu again received Rumania's highest decoration – the Order of *Mihai Viteazul* with Spades, Third Class – from King Michael himself. Despite a purge of royalist ARR personnel post-war, Ioan Milu remained with the air force for a few more years. In 1949, as a *Căpitan aviator*, he was a test pilot at the restructured

IAR factory in his native town, although he left the communist air force to return to civilian life soon afterwards. In 1980 Ioan Milu died in Brasov, the city of his birth, aged 72.

Dan Valentin Vizanty

Born on 9 February 1910 in Botosani, in northern Moldavia, to a wealthy family, Dan Valentin Vizanty was just 19 when he decided to enrol in the officers' flying school to become a flyer, rather than the artist his parents wanted him to be. Two years later, on 1 July 1931, he graduated with the rank of *Sublocotenent aviator*. Now qualified to fly reconnaissance biplanes like the Potez 25, Vizanty wished to transfer to the fighter arm, and on 16 October 1936 he was promoted to *Locotenent aviator* and assigned to *Flotila de luptā*, based at Bucharest-Pipera airfield.

Quickly mastering the PZL P.11 fighter, Vizanty soon became a patrol leader. Later, he was appointed deputy CO of *Escadrila 42 vânātoare* of *Grupul 3 vânātoare*. When the group was reorganised on 25 October 1939, *Escadrila 41 vânātoare* became *Escadrila 43 vânātoare*, and Vizanty was made its CO.

The unit was still equipped with obsolescent P.11s when Rumania went to war, and it commenced combat operations over Soviet-controlled Bessarabia from Bosanci airfield, near Suceava, in Bukovina. The first mention of Vizanty seeing any action came on 4 July, when a four-aircraft patrol bombed and strafed enemy artillery near Fālciu, east of the River Prut, with satisfactory results. Although the squadron had been involved in occasional dogfights with Soviet fighters, Vizanty did not fire his guns in anger until 17 September, when the squadron claimed a total of five confirmed and one unconfirmed kills over I-16s, plus a bomber, in the Tātarka area without loss. Vizanty was credited with an I-16 and an unidentified Soviet bomber destroyed.

By the time the campaign had ended, Vizanty had logged 51 combat sorties, and was credited with three victories out of an overall squadron tally of 22. He received the *Virtutea Aeronauticā cu 2 barete* and the Iron Cross, Second Class. The squadron returned to Rumania to be based at Galati. Shortly afterwards, Vizanty was appointed to a staff job at ARR headquarters, but a year later he resumed active duty as CO of *Grupul 6 vânātoare*. Equipped with the latest model of the Rumanian-made IAR 81C fighter, the group was based at Popesti-Leordeni airfield, near Bucharest. It was to defend the capital against the USAAF which had mounted Operation *Tidal Wave* on 1 August 1943, targeting the Ploiesti oilfields.

Combat with the new enemy started on 4 April 1944, when 350 B-17s and B-24s, with a weak P-38 fighter escort, attacked the Bucharest marshalling yards. With the escort separated from the bombers by ARR and Luftwaffe Bf 109G units, the IAR 81s could attack the heavy bombers with impunity. By the time the last American aircraft was south of the Danube, *Grupul 6 vânātoare* had claimed 16 bombers for just one loss. Vizanty was one of the victors, although his engine had been damaged by defensive fire from the bombers, compelling him to make a belly landing.

USAAF bombers returned the next day to raid the Ploiesti oilfields, and another 14 four-engined 'heavies' were claimed by the group, as well as two probables, this time without loss. The group CO was again reportedly among the victors, claiming another Liberator in the Bucharest area. On 6 June the group intercepted yet another attack on Ploiesti, but the Rumanians only achieved one kill – a B-17 shot down by Vizanty himself.

There were further encounters with the American intruders, with the peak being reached on 10 June, when the IAR 81s scrambled from their Popesti-Leordeni base and surprised a formation of P-38Js heading for Ploiesti. In the low-level dogfight which ensued, the Rumanians claimed to have shot down no less than 23 Lightnings for the loss of four IAR 81s. Vizanty claimed three P-38s, two of which were officially confirmed, but his aircraft, 'White 344', was damaged, although he able to return home.

By the time of their last encounter with the USAAF on 3 July 1944, pilots of *Grupul 6 vânătoare* had submitted confirmed claims for 87 enemy aircraft shot down. A further ten were unconfirmed, but 13 Rumanians had died in combat. Due to these heavy losses, all IAR 80/81 units were withdrawn from combat against the USAAF in early July and the group started to convert onto the superior Bf 109G-6, although training was not completed until the Rumanian about-face of 23 August 1944.

Group personnel – now incorporated into *Grupul 1 vânătoare,* but still commanded by Dan Vizanty – returned to combat after six long months, catching up with the fast-moving frontline in Slovakia in February 1945. By this time, Luftwaffe aircraft had become a rare sight, and there were no more aerial battles, preventing the 35-year-old *Lt c-dor av* Vizanty from increasing his overall score. Nevertheless, with 12 four-engined bombers allegedly amongst his tally, the ace's final tally stood at 43 victories – a truly outstanding achievement for a pilot flying the obsolete PZL P.11 and the IAR 80/81.

Vizanty received many decorations, including the coveted Order of *Michael the Brave,* Third Class. He was one of only three surviving officers flying the Rumanian-designed aircraft to receive this award, and the only recipient to participate in the fighting against the Americans.

Rumania's new communist rulers took a different view of Vizanty's accomplishments. As a result, an officer with over 17 years seniority and 4600 flying hours to his credit was compulsorily retired from the air force in August 1948. As a monarchist, he was considered unreliable and reactionary, and was jailed for five years for 'conspiracy against the social order'. After release, Vizanty's criminal record made it hard to get work, and he was forced into a variety of manual jobs such as gathering scrap metal, loading trucks and operating cranes.

In 1977, soon after retirement, Vizanty escaped from Rumania and defected to France, where he finally received the appreciation and respect denied him by his country. He married five times and fathered several children. Dan Valentin Vizanty, fourth ranking Rumanian ace, and top 'killer' of four-engined bombers, died in Paris on 2 November 1992, aged 82.

Cpt av Dan Vizanty was photographed just minutes after returning from a low-level dogfight with USAAF 71st FS P-38Js on 10 June 1944. He accounted for two of the 23 Lightings that his *Grupul 6 vânātoare* pilots claimed to have shot down that day. Behind him is his personal IAR 81C, 'White 344'

After conversion to the superior Bf 109G, the 35-year-old *Cpt av* Dan Vizanty returned to combat in February 1945 as CO of *Grupul 1 vânātoare*. However, he did not add to his score while flying the *Gustav* due to the lack of enemy action at this late stage of the war. But the record number of 12 four-engined USAAF bombers reportedly shot down by Vizanty elevated him to the position of fourth ranking ARR ace, and reportedly made him the highest scoring IAR 80/81 pilot with at least 43 victories

APPENDICES

APPENDIX A

THE RUMANIAN SCORING SYSTEM

In February 1944, the ARR introduced a new and unique system for attributing victories scored by its pilots over enemy aircraft. This included aircraft destroyed in the air or on the ground. As a result, credit for one or more victories could be awarded for an enemy aircraft destroyed according to the following system – one victory for a single-engined aircraft, two for a twin- or three-engined aircraft and three for a four- or six-engined aircraft destroyed, regardless of whether or not the claim was later officially confirmed.

When the system was introduced, individual scores were adjusted retroactively, and this often led to further confusion. For example, a pilot who shot down a B-17 Flying Fortress and a P-38 Lightning – such as *Cpt av* Petre Constantinescu of *Grupul 6 vânătoare* – became an instant five-victory ace. But an individual who destroyed four single-engined fighters in aerial combat – like *Lt av* Stefan Alexandrescu of *Grupul 8 vânătoare* – still cannot be considered an ace according to the unique ARR scoring system!

When several fighter pilots fired on the same target, and no clear victor could be established, each participant was credited with a full victory shared with the cell, patrol or squadron. However, only one victory counted towards the squadron's total tally (as with the French early-war system). These cases were extremely rare, however, since pilots resolved the issue among themselves before filing their official reports. Most such claims occurred in the 1941 campaign.

The Appendix B listing in this volume has been compiled according to the total number of ARR victories claimed. In cases where the number of victories scored is identical, the total of aircraft destroyed has been taken into consideration.

It is worth noting that by western standards, only 59 pilots would actually meet the normal criterion of five confirmed aircraft shot down in aerial combat.

It is estimated that Rumanian fighter pilots claimed approximately 1200 Soviet, American and German aircraft destroyed in the air or on the ground (claims from aircraft gunners or flak units have not been taken into account). This amounts to an estimated total of 1800 ARR victories according the unique Rumanian scoring system. The 126 aces claimed at least 1522 victories, which represents 85 per cent of the total claims made. In turn, over 100 *vânători* were killed in action.

Appendix B represents the first serious and thorough attempt to compile a comprehensive register of Rumanian fighter pilots who scored at least five victories under the ARR system. It is not considered to be truly definitive for several reasons, including a lack of complete and surviving documentation, the variety of individual claims and the confusing score accounting systems.

As no official list of aces exists, the table had to be compiled from individual claims, hence its imperfection. However, the author considers it to be reasonably accurate in view of the fact that an estimated 95 per cent of all claims submitted by ARR fighter pilots were discovered and processed.

The list of aces is based mainly on the following three official sources, in order of importance: firstly, Army and Air Force daily orders, in which victory claims were officially confirmed; secondly, combat diaries of various fighter units; and thirdly, *Monitorul Oficial*, the Rumanian Government's Official Gazette. Additionally, limited information was also gathered from numerous pilot logbooks, diaries and post-war memoirs.

APPENDIX B

ACES OF THE ARR (ROYAL RUMANIAN AIR FORCE), 1941-1945

Name	Rank (at last victory)	Unit(s)	Aircraft destroyed in air (confirmed)	Aircraft destroyed in air (unconfirmed)	Aircraft destroyed on ground	Total number of aircraft destroyed	Total number of ARR victories	Notes
Constantin Cantacuzino	Cpt rez av	Gr 5, 7 and 9 vân	42+1*	11	-	53+1*	69	Top scoring ARR ace overall. Oldest reserve fighter pilot, active on front (aged 40 in 1945). Seven victories against Axis. Flew 608 combat sorties and fought in 210 aerial battles; also, uniquely in ARR, flew 28 night combat sorties with a regular Bf 109G. Flew 45 transport sorties to front. Defected to west on 13 January 1948
Alexandru Şerbănescu †	Cpt av	Gr 7 and 9 vân	44	8	-	52	55	Top scoring ARR ace against Allies. Flew 590 combat sorties and participated in 235 aerial battles. KIA 18 August 1944, aged 32
Ioan Milu	Of ech cl III av	Gr 1, 7 and 9 vân	33	3+1*	1	37+1*	52	The ARR's oldest active fighter pilot, 43 in 1945. Flew 430 combat sorties and participated in 150 aerial battles by late July 1944. Over 500 combat sorties flown by May 1945. Twice shot down and WIA. Also credited with the destruction of T-34 tank
Dan Valentin Vizanty	Cpt av	Gr 1, 3 and 6 vân	15+1*	?	-	15+1*	43+	Flew 51 combat sorties in 1941. Total score based on secondary sources, with final tally uncertain due to lack of documents, but could be much lower. Reportedly shot down 12 four-engined US bombers flying IAR 80/81. Aged 35 in 1945. Family name alternatively spelled Vizante, or Vizanti. Defected to west in 1977
Constantin Rosariu	Lt av	Gr 7 vân	14	2	4	20	33	Flew 20 combat sorties at Stalingrad, 1942/43. Eight victories in campaign against Axis. Additional information from log book
Cristea Chirvăsuță	Adj av	Gr 7 and 9 vân	18	4	-	22	31	Highest ranking NCO ace, aged 30 in 1945
Ioan Maga	Of ech cl III av	Gr 5, 7 and 8 vân	15	5	-	20	29	Flew over 100 combat sorties in 1941. Total of about 200 combat sorties and fought in more than 50 aerial battles
Ioan Mucenica	Adj maj av	Gr 7 and 9 vân	21+1*	2	-	23+1*	27	Flew 450 combat sorties and participated in 150 aerial battles by 26 July 1944, when severely WIA
Vasile Gavriliu	Lt av	Gr 9 vân	14	2	4+1*	20+1*	27	Flew 306 combat sorties and 65 aerial battles. Three times crash-landed aircraft damaged in combat. Top-scoring ARR ace against Axis with 12 victories – primarily transports destroyed on ground. A total of 26 aircraft types flown during 13-year career as a pilot

Name	Rank	Group						Notes
Teodor Greceanu	Lt av	Gr 7 and 9 vân	18	5	1	24	24+	Flew 347 combat sorties and participated in 100+ aerial battles. Additional information from log book. Severely WIA 23 June 1944 and did not fight USAAF again
Constantin Lungulescu †	Adj rez av	Gr 7 and 9 vân	17+1*	2	-	19+1*	24+	Flew 376 combat sorties and fought in 96 aerial battles. KIA 24 June 1944
Ioan Di Cesare	Lt rez av	Gr 7 vân	16	3	?	19+	23+	Flew 210 combat sorties by late August 1943. Five 'efficient' ground attacks in 1941 but no official ground victories recorded. Family name alternatively spelled Dicezare
Dumitru Ilie	Adj maj av	Gr 6 and 8 vân	9	3	2	14	22	Flew 104 combat sorties and eight strafing missions in 1941, 19 fighter and four dive-bombing sorties at Stalingrad in 1942. Severely WIA on 23 June 1944 and did not fly operationally again. All victories were scored with IAR 80/81
Ioan Măiăcescu	Adj rez av	Gr 7 and 9 vân	16	3	-	19	21+	Flew 63 combat sorties in 1941. WIFA on 13 December 1944 and did not fly operationally again
Gheorghe Popescu-Ciocănel †	Cpt av	Gr 9 vân	13	1	-	14	19	Flew as short-range recce pilot in 1941. Over 200 combat sorties and more than 40 aerial battles. Downed in flames and severely burned on 26 July 1944 and died in hospital on 12 August
Dan Scurtu	Cpt av	Gr 7 vân	9	3	2	14	19+	Flew 256 combat sorties, 84 aerial battles, 14 strafing and eight dive-bombing missions
Teodor Zăbavă †	Adj av	Gr 8 vân and asalt	10+1*	3	4	17+1*	18+	Had flown 118 combat sorties by end October 1942. Transferred to Hs 129-equipped ground attack group in May 1943 to score final four kills. KIFA on 27 January 1944
Andrei Rădulescu	Adj sef av	Gr 5 and 9 vân	10	4	-	14	18	Severely WIA on 26 July 1944 and did not fly operationally again
Tiberiu Vinca †	Adj stag rez av	Gr 7 and 9 vân	12+1*	3	1	16+1*	17+	Flew 248 combat sorties. Killed in error by German He 111 gunners on 12 March 1944
Traian Dârjan †	Adj stag av	Gr 9 vân	11	1*	-	11+1*	17+	KIA by Luftwaffe on 25 February 1945 on 176th combat sortie – last ARR ace killed in aerial combat
Mihai Bulat	Slt av	Gr 4 and 6 vân	4+5*	-	-	4+5*	17	Flew 35 combat sorties in 1941
Ioan Nicola	Adj rez av	Gr 1, 3 and 6 vân	6+4*	-	-	6+4*	16	WIFA on 16 September 1944
Ion Dobran	Lt av	Gr 9 vân	9	3	1	13	15	Flew 340 combat sorties, fought in 74 aerial battles and shot down three times
Mihai Mihordea	Adj maj av	Gr 4 vân	9	1*	-	9+1*	15	-
Stefan Dumitrescu	Adj maj av	Gr 3 and 6 vân	6	2	-	8	15	Flew 77 combat sorties in 1941
Aurel Tifrea	Adj av	Gr 1 vân	4	1	1	6	15	WIA on 23 September 1944 and did not fly operationally again. Nine times shot down or involved in accidents. Flew 43 different aircraft. Family name Czifra, later changed to Rumanian Tifrea
Gheorghe Stănică †	Cpt av	Gr 2 vân	3	2	-	5	15	KIA on 18 May 1944
Eugen Fulga	Adj av	Gr 3 and 4 vân	3+6*	1*	-	3+7*	15	-

Name	Rank	Group(s)					Total	Notes
Ernst Stengl *	Uffz (Luftwaffe)	Gr 9 vân	11	-	1	12	14+	* Luftwaffe pilot assigned to Gr 9 vân as liaison officer from February 1944. Flew combat sorties with Rumanian comrades often in Rumanian-marked Bf 109Gs. Score appears in official Rumanian victory listings. By end July 1944, he had flown 120 combat sorties with the group. Served with 6th, 8th and 11th Staffeln of JG 52. Destroyed 17 aircraft in total
Evghenie (Eugen) Camencianu †	Adj stag av	Gr 5 vân	7	3	-	10	14+	Flew 73 combat sorties in 1941. KIFA on 5 October 1942
Constantin Popescu	Adj av	Gr 1 and 6 vân	7	1	-	8	14+	-
Petre Cojocaru	Adj av	Gr 2 vân	3+1*	1	-	4+1*	14	Flew 60 combat sorties in 1941
Dumitru Chera	Adj stag av	Gr 1 and 6 vân	4+1*	-	2^	4+1* [+2^]	13 [+3^]	^ Unauthorised strafing of enemy airfield and two victories not claimed and not entered in combat reports
Iosif Moraru	Adj stag rez av	Gr 7 and 9 vân	7	4	1	12	13+	-
Ioan Micu	Cpt av	Gr 8 and 9 vân	7+1*	1	3	11+1*	13	Flew 112 combat sorties and five strafing missions in 1941. Shot down eight aircraft in only ten aerial battles
Mircea Dumitrescu	Lt av	Gr 3 and 6 vân	6+2*	1+1*	-	7+3*	13	Four times posted MIA and returned
Horia Agarici	Cpt av	Gr 5 and 7 vân	6	2	-	8	13	-
Lucian Toma †	Cpt av	Gr 5, 7 and 9 vân	7	-	-	7	13+	Flew 86 combat sorties and 112 hours in 1941. KIA on 25 September 1944
Hariton Dusescu	Lt av	Gr 7 and 9 vân	9	1	1	11	12	Flew 360 combat sorties and fought 60+ aerial battles by late July 1944. His aircraft was hit nine times in aerial combat
Gheorghe Tutuianu	Adj av	Gr 8 vân	8	2	-	10	12+	-
Ion Galea	Lt av	Gr 5 and 9 vân	5	2	-	7	12+	Total based on memoirs
Gheorghe Cristea †	Slt av	Gr 1 vân	3+1*	-	-	3+1*	12	KIA on 18 May 1944
Ioan Bârlădeanu †	Lt av	Gr 1 vân	2+1*	1	-	3+1*	12	Flew 74 combat sorties in 1941. KIA on 31 May 1944
Nicolae Polizu †	Lt rez av	Gr 7 vân	10	-	-	10	11	Flew 97 combat sorties and fought 45 aerial combats. KIA on 6 (or 2) May 1943
Stefan Greceanu	Adj stag rez av	Gr 7 vân	7	3	-	10	11	Flew 78 combat sorties in 1941
Ioan Panaite †	Adj maj av	Gr 7 and 9 vân	8	1	-	9	11	Flew 92 combat sorties and 104 hours to 7 October 1942 when WIA by flak. Returned to combat early 1943 and KIA on 10 August 1944
Constantin Ursache	Adj av	Gr 5, 7 and 9 vân	8	1	-	9	11	Flew 33 combat sorties and fought five aerial combats on Stalingrad front. Family name also spelled Ursachi
Florian Alexiu †	Lt av	Gr 8 vân	5	1	2	8	11+	Flew 113 combat sorties up to 18 September 1942, when WIA by Soviet bombs on Tuzov airfield – died next day. One of the most active fighter pilots of 1941 campaign with 104 sorties and eight strafing missions. Downed five aircraft in nine aerial battles
Cristu I Cristu	Lt av	Gr 3 and 4 vân	4+4*	-	-	4+4*	11	-
Stefan Octavian Ciutac	Slt av	Gr 7 and 9 vân	5	-	1	6	11	Additional information from memoirs
Nicolae Macri	Adj av	Gr 3 and 4 vân	5	-	-	5	11	-
Ioan Ivancievici †	Lt av	Gr 3 and 4 vân	2+3*	2	-	4+3*	11	Flew 76 combat sorties in 1941. KIA on 25 September 1944
Niculae Burileanu	Adj sef av	Gr 7 vân	8	1	1	10	10+	Flew 70 combat sorties in 1941. Aged 36 in 1945. Flew 50 types in 32-year career as pilot

Name	Rank	Unit						Notes
Liviu Muresan †	Slt av	Gr 7 vân	7	2	-	9	10	Flew 30 combat sorties and fought in two aerial combats over Stalingrad 1942/43. KIA on 10 October 1943
Laurentiu Catană *	Adj av	Gr 7 vân	7	-	1	8	10	* PoW after colliding with Soviet Spitfire on 26 June 1943. Returned after seven years imprisonment in USSR
Emil Băian †	Adj stag av	Gr 9 vân	5	2	-	7	10	KIA on 26 July 1944
Ioan Dimache	Adj av	Gr 3 and 6 vân	6+1*	-	-	6+1*	10	-
Mircea Mazilu	Adj stag av	Gr 3 and 7 vân	2+2*	3	-	5+2*	10+	Flew 80 combat sorties in 1941
Constantin Dimache †	Adj av	Gr 4 and 6 vân	4+3*	-	-	4+3*	10	KIA on 23 June 1944
Dumitru Baciu	Lt av	Gr 1 and 6 vân	4 +1**	1+1*	1^	5+1*+1^	10 (+3)	^ Unauthorised strafing of enemy airfield, kill not claimed and not entered in combat reports. **Yak fighter shot down 4 May 1945 not confirmed either. Attacked and wounded by hijackers in August 1948 while delivering mail in Po-2. Died in hospital six months later
Gheorghe Hăpăianu †	Adj maj av	Gr 4 and 7 vân	7	2	-	9	9	KIA on 15 July 1944
Florian Budu †	Adj stag av	Gr 6 and 8 vân	7	-	2	9	9	Flew 85 combat sorties in 1941. KIA on 31 May 1944
Parsifal Ştefănescu †	Lt av	Gr 5 and 8 vân	7	-	-	7	9	Flew 58 combat sorties in 1941. KIA on 28 June 1944
Petre Cordescu	Adj stag av	Gr 5 vân	6	-	-	6	9	Flew 41 combat sorties in 1941, and scored only in 1941. Defected to Turkey on 29 August 1944 in a Hurricane
Alexandru Moldoveanu	Adj av	Gr 7 vân	4	2	-	6	9	Flew 51 combat sorties in 1941
Mircea Senchea	Lt av	Gr 9 vân	3	3	-	6	9	-
Gheorghe Prasinopol †	Adj sef av	Gr 1 vân	3	-	-	3	9	Severely WIA on 28 June 1944 and died the following day
Constantin Baltă	Slt av	Sc de vân**	2	1	-	3	9	**Fighter school at Brasov. Esc 44 vân, 40 combat missions
Constantin Georgescu	Cpt av	Gr 1 vân	2	1	-	3	9	-
Petre Mihăilescu †	Slt av	Gr 1 vân	2	1	-	3	9	KIA on 23 September 1944
Gheorghe Mociorniţă †	Slt av	Gr 1 and 2 vân	2	1	-	3	9	KIA by ground fire on 21 April 1945 – the last ARR ace to die in action
Jean (Ioan) Sandru	Slt av	Gr 7 vân	2	1	-	3	9	-
Ioan Sandu †	Cpt c-dor av	Gr 1 vân	2	1	-	3	9	Highest ranking ARR pilot to be KIA, on 23 June 1944
Panait Grigore †	Slt av	Gr 1 vân	1	2	-	3	9	KIFA on 5 May 1944
Constantin Nicoară	Adj av	Gr 7 and 9 vân	5	2	-	7	8	Made last ARR victory claim of war (Bf 109K) over Slovakia on 1 April 1945
Gheorghe Cocebas	Adj av	Gr 6 and 8 vân	6	-	-	6	8	Flew 61 combat sorties in 1941. Severely WIA on 23 June 1944 and did not fly operationally again
Emil Georgescu	Cpt av	Gr 5 vân	4	1	-	5	8	Flew 50 combat sorties in 1941, and scored only in 1941
Stefan Pucas	Adj sef av	Gr 8 vân and asalt	4	1	-	5	8	Flew 66 combat sorties in 1941. From May 1943 was Hs 129 ground attack pilot
Ioan Marinciu	Adj av	Gr. 7 and 9 vân	4	-	-	4	8	WIA on 23 December 1944 and did not fly operationally again
Gheorghe Alexandru Grecu	Adj av	Gr 2 and 4 vân	3	1*	-	3+1*	8	All confirmed kills during campaign against Axis, including defecting Rumanian Hs 129B
Carol Anastasescu	Lt av	Gr 6 vân	2	1	-	3	8	-
Vasile Fortu †	Slt av	Gr 8 vân	4	2	1	7	7+	Flew 101 combat sorties and fought in 11 aerial battles in 1941. KIFA on 4 September 1942

Name	Rank	Group						Notes
Ioan Florea	Adj av	Gr 3 and 7 vân	5	-	-	5	7	Scored one of very few ARR kills by ramming (I-16) on 28 August 1941
Constantin Pomut †	Adj stag rez av	Gr 5 and 7 vân	4	1	-	5	7	Flew 59 combat sorties in 1941. KIA on 10 January 1944
Vasile Mirilă	Adj sef av	Gr 1 and 8 vân	3	-	1	4	7	Flew 39 combat sorties in 1941
Aurel Vlădăreanu	Adj av	Gr 6 vân	3	-	-	3	7	Family name also listed as Vlădărescu
Titus Gheorghe Ionescu †	Lt av	Gr 3 and 4 vân	2	1	-	3	7	Flew 73 combat sorties in 1941. KIA on 29 September 1944
Erich Richard Selei	Slt rez av	Gr 8 vân	5	1	-	6	6	Flew 57 combat sorties in 1941. WIFA on 28 May 1942 and did not fly operationally again
Ioan Vonica †	Slt av	Gr 8 vân	5	-	1	6	6	Flew 41 combat sorties and fought in five aerial combats until WIA on 27 August 1941. He died ten days later in hospital. First ace KIA
Radu Reinek	Lt rez av	Gr 8 vân	5+1*	-	-	5+1*	6	-
Constantin Popescu	Adj stag av	Gr 5 vân	5	-	-	5	6	Flew 56 combat sorties in 1941
Iuliu Anca	Slt av	Gr 8 vân	4	1	-	5	6	-
Pavel Turcanu †	Adj av	Gr 9 vân	4	-	1	5	6	KIA on 26 July 1944
Nicolae Naghirneac	Lt av	Gr 7 and 9 vân	2	2	-	4	6	Flew 25 combat sorties and fought in five aerial combats at Stalingrad in 1942/43
Iosif Chiuhulescu †	Adj stag rez av	Gr 3 vân	1+3*	1	-	2+3*	6	KIA on 16 September 1944
Dumitru Niculescu †	Adj stag av	Gr 3 vân	2+3*	-	-	2+3*	6	Scored only in 1941. KIA on 24 December 1944
Stefan Florescu	Lt av	Gr 1 and 5 vân	3	-	-	3	6+	Scored last kill against Allies (VVS Pe-2) on 24 August 1944
Eugen Taflan	Adj av	Gr 4 and 7 vân	2	1	-	3	6	WIA by flak on 2 April 1945 and did not fly operationally again
Virgil Angelescu	Adj stag av	Gr 1 vân	2	-	-	2	6	-
Pavel Bucsa	Slt av	Gr 6 vân	2	-	-	2	6	WIA on 7 May 1944 and did not fly operationally again
Vasile Ionită	Adj av	Gr 4 vân	1	1	-	2	6	-
Mircea Teodorescu	Lt av	Gr 1 vân	1	1	-	2	6	-
Gheorghe Gulan	Slt av	Gr 1 vân	1+1*	-	?	1+1*	6+	Flew 36 combat sorties and fought in 18 aerial battles against USAAF. Force-landed or returned to base with IAR 81 damaged in dogfights seven times. Personal aircraft showed three ground victory markings, but no official confirmation of victories has been found
Andrei Marulis	Adj av	Gr 1 vân	1+1*	-	-	1+1*	6	
Petre Scurtu †	Slt av	Gr 8 vân	2*	-	-	2*	6	KIA on 31 May 1944
Vintila Brătianu	Slt rez av	Gr 7 vân	5	-	-	5	5+	Flew 109 combat sorties by end of 1942. Defected to west on 19 May 1947
Mihai Belcin	Adj av	Gr 6 vân	4+1*	1	-	4+1*	5+	Score based on memoirs. Ju 87D Stuka pilot from March 1943
Florea Iordache †	Adj av	Gr 7 vân	4	1	-	5	5	KIA on 14 September 1943
Ioan Mihăilescu †	Slt av	Gr 8 vân	4	1	-	5	5	Flown 106 combat sorties by 18 September 1942, when WIA by Soviet bombs on Tuzov airfield. Died next day
Emil Droc	Cpt av	Gr 6 vân	3	2	-	5	5	IAR test pilot. Only one combat assignment, to Stalingrad, in late 1942, when he flew 42 combat missions aged 39. During 26-year career as pilot he flew 59 aircraft types (4120 flying hours and 10,290 landings)
Costin Miron	Adj stag av	Gr 7 and 9 vân	3	2	-	5	5	-

Name	Rank	Group						Notes
Romeo Neacsu	Adj stag av	Gr 3 and 7 vân	3	2	-	5	5	Privately claims 18 aircraft shot down and 2500 hours flown, but not confirmed officially. Hijacked commercial flight and defected in 1947
Ioan Bocsan	Lt av	Gr 7 vân	3	-	2+	5+	5+	-
Marin Ghica †	Cpt av	Gr 5 vân	3	-	2	5	5+	Flew 65 combat sorties in 1941 with 15 aerial battles. KIA on 1 August 1943. One source mentions that the B-24D Ghica attacked on last sortie eventually crashed, but with no witness to confirm the 'kill' it is not counted in the final tally
Ioan Simionescu	Lt rez av	Gr 7 and 9 vân	4	?	-	4+	5+	Flew 320 combat sorties by late July 1944
Alexandru Economu †	Adj av	Gr 7 and 9 vân	3	1	-	4	5	KIA on 26 July 1944
Nicolae Sculey Logotheti	Serg TR av	Gr 5 and 8 vân	3	1	-	4	5	Flew 29 combat sorties in 1941
Nicolae Iolu	Adj sef av	Gr 7 vân	3	-	1	4	5	Flew 70 combat sorties in 1941
Gheorghe Pisoschi †	Adj av	Gr 6 vân	2+1*	1	-	3+1*	5	KIA on 24 November 1942
Dumitru Encioiu	Adj av	Gr 9 vân	3	-	-	3	5	WIA on 8 August 1944 and did not fly operationally again
Ioan Rosescu †	Cpt av	Gr 5 vân	3	-	-	3	5	6 combat sorties and 3 aerial combats until KIA on 12 September 1941
Nicolae Bătrânu	Lt av	Gr 7 and 9 vân	2	1	-	3	5	WIFA on 5 May 1944 and did not fly operationally again
Vasile Pascu	Adj stag rez av	Gr 8 vân and asalt	2	1*	-	2+1*	5	Flew 225 combat sorties, 90 as fighter pilot. Score includes claim for Operation HALPRO B-24D on 12 June 1942, shared with German pilot. Hs 129 pilot from May 1943. WIA on 15 April 1945 and did not fly again
Clemente Muresan	Lt av	Gr 2 vân	2	-	-	2	5	Information from memoirs. No official confirmation found so far
Petre Constantinescu	Cpt av	Gr 6 vân	1	1	-	2	5	-
Alexandru Manoliu †	Cpt av	Gr 7 vân	1	-	4	5	5+	KIA on 12 September 1942

Key

† – killed in line of duty (42 out of the 126 'ace' pilots, or one in three, killed)

KIA – killed in action

KIFA – killed in flying accident

MIA – missing in action

PoW – prisoner of war

WIA – wounded in action

WIFA – wounded in flying accident

* – victory shared with other members of the combat formation in which the claimant was part of – usually the patrulă (patrol, a four-aircraft fighter formation). In this case, the patrol's four pilots received a shared victory each for every enemy aircraft destroyed during that particular aerial combat

91

Colour Plates

1

He 112B 'Black 13' Wk-Nr. 2044 of *Sublocotenent aviator* (Pilot Officer) Teodor Moscu, *Escadrila 51 vânătoare, Grupul 5 vânătoare*, Focsani-North, 22 June 1941

Moscu scored one of the ARR's first aerial victories of World War 2 when, during a raid on the Soviet airfield of Bulgărica, in southern Bessarabia, he claimed two kills, plus a probable, which represented his sole victories. Few combat kills were scored by pilots flying the sleek and manoeuvrable, but underpowered, He 112, as the sole group equipped with the aircraft was tasked with flying ground support rather than fighter missions. Note Walt Disney's 'Pluto' squadron emblem.

2

Hurricane Mk I 'Yellow 3' of *Locotenent aviator* (Flying Officer) Horia Agarici, independent *Escadrila 53 vânătoare*, Mamaia, 23 June 1941

After his triple score on the second day of Rumania's war against the Soviet Union, Agarici became a living legend and folk hero among his compatriots, although his final score of five confirmed kills and two probables (equivalent to 12 victories under the Rumanian scoring system) shows that despite his sudden fame, he was not among the ARR's high-scoring aces. His Hurricane retained the original RAF camouflage scheme, including wing undersurfaces painted half white and half black. Besides standard yellow propeller tips, two additional coloured stripes – believed to be red and yellow – were brush-painted on the blades. Note the mounted 'Mickey Mouse' with lance squadron emblem (a similar motif later appeared on IAR 80s, as well as on Bf 109G-2/G-4s of *Escadrila 53 vânătoare, Grupul 7 vânătoare*) and the seldom-used, stencilled style, King Michael's cross national markings. The latter were applied only on Hurricanes and He 111H-3s (wings only), and occasionally on Blenheims, Potez 633s and early-production Bf 109 *Gustavs*.

3

P.11F 'White 102' of *Adjutant stagiar aviator* (Lance Corporal) Vasile Cotoi, *Escadrila 44 vânătoare, Grupul 3 vânătoare*, Bessarabia, July 1941

Cotoi was shot down and killed while flying this aircraft in combat with six I-16s near Freudenthal, in south-western Ukraine, on 2 September 1941. By then he had been credited with three confirmed victories and one probable during the course of 48 combat sorties, the last of which was over a *Rata* just before he was shot down.

4

Hurricane Mk I 'Yellow 5' of *Adjutant sef aviator* (Flight Sergeant) Andrei Rădulescu, *Escadrila 53 vânătoare*, Salz, July 1941

Rădulescu became the top scoring ARR ace in the first Rumanian campaign with seven Soviet aircraft confirmed shot down, as well as four probables. These kills represented at least 14 victories under the ARR scoring system. Like all other Rumanian Hurricanes, 'Yellow 5' retained its original RAF camouflage scheme at this early stage of the war.

Although the Michael's Cross national marking was applied to the fuselage, the pre-May 1941 cockade was retained on the wing undersurfaces, which may have been due to a recent wing exchange.

5

P.24P 'White 24' of *Adjutant stagiar aviator* (Lance Corporal) Costin Popescu, *Escadrila 62 vânătoare, Grupul 6 vânătoare*, Bucharest-Pipera, mid-September 1941

Popescu survived the ARR's 1941 Bessarabian campaign with a score of three kills, making him one of the most successful of all P.24 pilots. The Polish fighter equipped *Grupul 6 vânătoare*, and despite its obsolescence, performed well against unescorted Soviet bombers and outdated biplane fighters like the I-153.

6

He 112B 'White 24' Wk-Nr. 2055, *Escadrila 52 vânătoare, Grupul 5 vânătoare*, Komrat-South, early August 1941

Warrant Officer 3rd Grade Ioan Maga, eighth-ranking scorer in the ARR's 1941 campaign, cut his teeth on the He 112, scoring the first of his 29 victories over a Soviet fighter (reported to be a 'Seversky', but more likely a MiG-3) at Yeremievka on 1 August 1941. 'White 24' survived the campaign, but was lost soon afterwards in a training accident.

7

P.11F 'White 122' of *Sublocotenent aviator de rezervă* (Reserve Pilot Officer) Cristu I Cristu, *Grupul 3 vânătoare*, Odessa, late September 1941

During the 1941 campaign, Cristu was credited with three kills, plus another four shared. After an overhaul, this aircraft was repainted in the typical Rumanian military aircraft colour scheme of dark green over light blue. Flying an IAR 80C on 1 August 1943, Cristu shot down a B-24D Liberator which was attacking the oilfields at Ploiesti during Operation *Tidal Wave*. His final score was 11 victories.

8

IAR 80 'White 42' of *Grupul 8 vânătoare*, Bessarabia, August 1941

With no IAR 80 pilot succeeding in scoring as many as 13 victories during the 1941 campaign, the markings on this aircraft probably denote either the total score of the pilots who flew it, or the squadron tally. Another possibility is that the victory markings were chalked on the aircraft for the benefit of a visiting ARR propaganda photographer. This aircraft survived four long years of war, eventually ending its days at a pilots' school.

9

Bf 109E-3 'Yellow 35' Wk-Nr. 2480 of *Grupul 7 vânătoare, Escadrila 58 vânătoare*, Kishinev (Chisinău), late July 1941

This aircraft was often flown by *Sublocotenent aviator de rezervă* Ion Simionescu, who completed the ARR's 1941 campaign with two Soviet aircraft confirmed as shot down. He would add more victories to his score, and end the war with at least five kills. Note the single victory bar, painted just aft of the air intake, and the 'Donald Duck' emblem, which was exclusively applied to the group's *Emils*.

10

IAR 80A 'White 86' of *Locotenent aviator* (Flying Officer) Ioan Micu, *Escadrila 41 vânătoare, Grupul 8 vânătoare*, southern Bessarabia, July 1941

Micu was the highest scoring IAR 80 pilot of the ARR's 1941 campaign with at least 11 victories to his credit, eight of these being claimed during the course of just ten aerial engagements. On 18 May 1944, Micu claimed a P-38 Lightning to take his final score to 13 victories.

11

Bf 109E-3 'Yellow 26' of *Adjutant stagiar de rezervă aviator* (Reserve Lance Corporal) Stefan Greceanu, *Grupul 7 vânătoare, Escadrila 57 vânătoare*, Salz, Bessarabia, early September 1941

The name *Nadia II* was applied in white to the yellow-painted engine cowling, the Roman numeral 'II' indicating that this was Greceanu second aircraft, the first having been lost in combat. Greceanu ended the Bessarabian campaign an ace, credited with six aircraft destroyed. 'Yellow 26' was set on fire and burnt out on 22 September 1941, when Soviet I-16s of the 69th IAP strafed Salz airfield.

12

Bf 109E-3 'Yellow 11' Wk-Nr. 2729 of *Locotenent aviator* Alexandru Serbănescu, *Grupul 7 vânătoare*, Bucharest-Pipera, late summer 1942

Serbănescu was to become the ARR's top ace whilst Rumania was allied to the Axis cause, but the six victory bars painted underneath the windscreen of this particular *Emil* do not represent his claims, as he was still a novice at this stage. The personal nickname *Adrian* has been painted in white on the Axis-yellow engine cowling. The spinner was a quarter white and three-quarters black to conform with *Luftflotte 4* standards. However, the reasoning behind the fighter's red rudder top remains a mystery. This E-3 was transformed into an 'assault' E-4B/U2 in April 1943, and the aircraft survived the war and was eventually written off in the late 1940s.

13

IAR 80B 'White 199', of *Căpitan aviator* (Flight Lieutenant) Emil Frideric Droc, CO of *Escadrila 60 vânătoare, Grupul 8 vânătoare*, Stalingrad area, September 1942

A test pilot at the IAR works, 39-year-old Droc volunteered for frontline service in 1942 and was appointed CO of the 60th FS at Stalingrad in September of that year. He flew 42 combat sorties during his four-month-long stint in the frontline, being credited with three individual aerial victories (two Yaks and a MiG-3), one probable (a MiG-3) and one ground victory (an unidentified single-engined aircraft) during that time. His four aerial victories were symbolised by four 'Vs' painted on the fin of his personal mount. 'White 199' was destroyed at Tuzov airfield by a lone Soviet bomber on 19 September 1942.

14

Bf 109E-7 'Yellow 64' Wk-Nr. 704 of *Adjutant aviator de rezervă* Tiberiu Vinca, *Grupul 7 vânătoare*, Stalingrad, late 1942

An ace with 13 kills to his credit, Vinca was shot down in error by a Luftwaffe bomber gunner in March 1944. Note the five victory bars, the name *Nella* on the cowling, the pilot's initials and the chalked-on inscription of the Rumanians' final objective. This refurbished ex-Luftwaffe aircraft was one of the few *Emils* sent to Stalingrad which returned to Rumania in early 1943. It was later handed over to *Escadrila 52 vânătoare* to protect the important Cernavodă bridge, over the River Danube, and Constanta harbour.

15

Bf 109G-2 'White 8' (believed to be Wk-Nr. 10360) of *Adjutant aviator de rezervă* Stefan 'Bebe' Greceanu, *Escadrila 53 vânătoare*, Mizil, July 1943

This machine is believed to have been the personal aircraft of *Adjutant aviator de rezervă* Stefan 'Bebe' Greceanu, an ace with 11 victories, who was attached to the joint German-Rumanian unit I./JG 4.

16

Bf 109G-4 'White 4' Wk-Nr. 19546, of *Căpitan de rezervă aviator* (Reserve Flight Lieutenant) Constantin Cantacuzino, CO of *Escadrila 58 vânătoare, Grupul 7 vânătoare*, southern Ukraine, summer 1943

Cantacuzino was alone on 29 June 1943 when he encountered a four-aircraft patrol of red-nosed Soviet Spitfires near Alexandrovka. He shot down two of them before the others damaged the *Gustav* so badly that the Rumanian pilot had to belly land his burning fighter in friendly territory, escaping unharmed. Prince 'Bâzu' Cantacuzino ended the war as the top-scoring Rumanian ace with 69 victories. As this aircraft clearly shows, most Bf 109G-2s and G-4s loaned to the ARR by the Luftwaffe for frontline use had their original three-tone grey colours over-painted on the top surfaces with the ARR's dark green.

17

IAR 80C 'White 279' of *Locotenent aviator* (Flying Officer) Ion Bârlădeanu, CO of *Escadrila 45 vânătoare, Grupul 4 vânătoare*, Târgsorul Nou airfield, near Ploiesti, August 1943

In his first encounter with the USAAF on 1 August 1943, Bârlădeanu scored two kills against B-24Ds participating in Operation *Tidal Wave*. He would subsequently shoot down two more B-24s (the first on 21 April 1944, shared with his patrol, and the second exactly two weeks later), which remained unconfirmed. Bârlădeanu was killed on 31 May 1944 when he was shot down by USAAF fighters over Clejani-Rusii while returning to his base. The two vertical stripes below the cockpit of this machine symbolise his B-24 kills of 1 August 1943. Note Bârlădeanu's personal emblem in front of the cockpit. 'White 279' was destroyed at Saki airfield, in southern Ukraine, by retreating Rumanian troops on 15 April 1944.

18

Bf 109G-2 'White 1' (believed to be Wk-Nr. 14680) of *Escadrila 53 vânătoare*, attached to the joint German-Rumanian I./JG 4, Mizil, August 1943

Although this aircraft was the usual mount of unit CO *Căpitan aviator* Lucian Toma, it was hastily taken into combat against

Operation *Tidal Wave* B-24s by *Adjutant aviator* Dumitru Encioiu on 1 August 1943. He managed to down a Liberator, but his engine's cooling system was damaged by return fire from his target, compelling Encioiu to belly land his *Gustav* in a maze field. The following summer, 'Mitrică' Encioiu 'bagged' two Mustangs, raising his overall score to five ARR victories. Note the seven black victory bars on the white rudder, each symbolising a Soviet aircraft downed by Toma, and the mounted 'Mickey Mouse' with lance squadron emblem.

19

Bf 110C-1 'Black 2Z+EW' Wk-Nr. 1819, of 12./NJG 6 (Luftwaffe unit designation), referred to in Rumanian documents as *Escadrila 51 vânătoare de noapte*, Ploiesti, 1 August 1943

Căpitan aviator Prince Marin Ghica, CO of the German-Rumanian nightfighter squadron, met his death while flying this Bf 110 during an attack on USAAF B-24Ds in daylight during *Tidal Wave*. He and his radio operator/rear gunner, *Submaistru RTFF mitralior* Gheorghe Teliban, baled out, but the pilot's parachute did not open. Ghica is believed to have destroyed the B-24 that he had attacked from close range, and whose rear gunner fatally damaged the Bf 110. However, the kill was not witnessed. Even without these three possible victories, the 34-year-old pilot was already an ace by Rumanian standards.

20

Bf 109E-3 'Yellow 45' Wk-Nr. 2731 of *Căpitan aviator* Gheorghe Iliescu, CO of *Grupul 5 vânătoare, Escadrila 52 vânătoare*, Mamaia, summer 1943

Iliescu's usual aircraft, this heavily weathered machine displays the girl's name *Ileana* in white on the Axis-yellow engine cowling. The veteran *Emil* soldiered on throughout the ARR's first two campaigns on the eastern front, before ending its operational days patrolling the shores of the Black Sea in search of Soviet intruders.

21

Hs 129B-2 'White 126a' Wk-Nr. 141274 of *Adjutant aviator* (Corporal) Teodor Zăbavă, *Grupul 8 asalt* (8th Assault Group), October 1943

Zăbavă shot down a Yak fighter near Eigenfeld on 25 October 1943 in this machine (one of four victories credited to him in the Hs 129), although the bulk of his kills were claimed flying IAR 80s. According to Rumanian archives, this somewhat enigmatic pilot – no photograph of him has yet come to light – was actually the third-ranking IAR 80 ace with ten enemy aircraft confirmed as shot down, one unconfirmed and one shared, plus one destroyed on the ground. Zăbavă died (as a passenger) in an aircraft accident on 29 January 1944.

22

Bf 109E-4 'Yellow 47' Wk-Nr. 2643 of *Sublocotenent aviator* (Pilot Officer) Ion Galea, *Grupul 5 vânătoare, Escadrila 52 vânătoare*, Mamaia, late 1943

The pilot's initials – I G – can be seen painted in white on the fighter's yellow engine cowling. Note also the small victory bars that adorn the fin in place of the swastika, these markings contrasting with victory symbols applied to other *Grupul 7 vânătoare* Bf 109Es at this time, which typically took the form of thicker oblique bars beneath the windscreen (see profile 14). Galea's first three kills were two Pe-2 bomber/reconnaissance machines and a Yakovlev fighter, all scored in the Mamaia-Cernavodă-Constanta area in 1943. He ended the war with five kills confirmed and two unconfirmed, which were equivalent to at least a dozen victories when the ARR scoring system was applied.

23

IAR 81C 'White 341' of *Sublocotenent aviator* (Pilot Officer) Dumitru 'Take' Baciu, *Grupul 6 vânătoare*, Popesti-Leordeni, February 1944

By the time 'Take' Baciu was assigned this IAR 81C in early 1944, he already had three victories to his name – a Yak downed on 20 December 1942 near Stalingrad and an unidentified Soviet twin-engined bomber claimed later that same day, which remained unconfirmed. During the summer of 1944, Baciu would shoot down two USAAF aircraft (a P-38 Lightning on 10 May and a B-17 Flying Fortress on 23 June), thereby gaining five more victories. During the ARR's anti-Axis campaign, Baciu – promoted to *Locotenent* – was credited with destroying a German Bf 109G on 23 September 1944. He was one of only three IAR 80/81 pilots to achieve this rare feat. Baciu may have scored the final Rumanian aerial victory of the war over a (nominally) allied Soviet Yak fighter, which attacked his two-Bf 109G element over Czechoslovakia on 4 May 1945. He was himself shot down during the skirmish, although he emerged from the incident unhurt. Baciu's victory was never officially acknowledged, having only been discovered in recent research by the author for this book. Note Baciu's personal emblem, Walt Disney's 'Bambi', painted in great detail on the engine cowling.

24

Bf 109G-4 'White J' of *Căpitan aviator* (Flight Lieutenant) Dan Scurtu, *Escadrila 57 vânătoare, Grupul 7 vânătoare*, Leipzig, Bessarabia, late April 1944

Scurtu was one of the group's 'old hands', and by the end of the war the 31-year-old pilot was credited with nine enemy aircraft confirmed shot down, with an additional three unconfirmed, during the course of 84 aerial battles. His aircraft carried a letter instead of the regular numeral, which was painted onto the fin rather than the fuselage, as was typical of the *Gustavs* assigned to *Escadrila 57 vânătoare*. The camouflage scheme worn by this particular Bf 109G was also unusual.

25

IAR 80A 'White 97' of *Adjutant aviator* (Corporal) Dumitru Chera, *Grupul 1 vânătoare*, Ploiesti, 5 May 1944

On 5 May 1944, Chera engaged and shot down a B-24 near Ploiesti, and he would go on to score twice more against USAAF four-engined bombers on 7 and 18 May. After the Rumanians changed sides on 23 August 1944, 'Mitică' Chera joined *Escadrila 65 vânătoare, Grupul 6 vânătoare*. To avenge the death of his comrades killed by Luftwaffe pilots, he flew as wingman to the pugnacious 'Take' Baciu in an unauthorised strafing mission against an Axis airfield north of Turda (Torda/Thorenburg) in the late afternoon of 23 September 1944. Upon returning from the mission, each pilot claimed a He 111H destroyed on the ground, while Chera also stated that he had left a taxiing Fw 190 ablaze. These results were not officially acknowledged, however. Not counting this 'private venture', Chera's final score was 13 victories.

26
IAR 81C 'White 344' of Căpitan aviator (Flight Lieutenant) Dan-Valentin Vizanty, CO of Grupul 6 vânătoare, Popesti-Leordeni airfield, 10 June 1944

Flying this aircraft, 34-year-old Vizanty led his unit against low-flying P-38Js of the 71st FS/1st FG. During the ensuing melee, Vizanty was credited with two Lightnings shot down. He reportedly became the top-scoring IAR 80/81 pilot, and the ARR's fourth-ranking ace, with at least 43 victories. Vizanty was also the most successful pilot against USAAF four-engined bombers, claiming 12 kills.

27
Bf 109G-6 'White 2' (possibly Wk-Nr. 166161) of Escadrila 47 vânătoare, Grupul 9 vânătoare, July 1944

This aircraft was reputedly being flown by squadron CO, Căpitan aviator Gheorghe Popescu-Ciocănel, when he was shot down over Tecuci in combat with Fifteenth Air Force P-51s on 26 July 1944. Badly-burned, Popescu-Ciocănel died ten days later in the local hospital, by which time he was credited with 13 confirmed and one unconfirmed aircraft downed in 40+ aerial combats. Note the Grupul 9 vânătoare Deßloch–Serbănescu emblem on the engine cowling.

28
Bf 109G-6 'Yellow 1' of Căpitan aviator Alexandru Serbănescu, CO Grupul 9 vânătoare, August 1944

On 4 August 1944, Serbănescu shot down his final victim – a P-51 from the 52nd FG – to take his overall score to 55 victories, and make him the second ranking ARR ace. He was subsequently killed while flying this aircraft when he was bounced by Mustangs on 18 August 1944 near Brasov.

29
IAR 81C 'White 343' of Adjutant sef aviator (Flight Sergeant) Vasile Mirilă, Grupul 2 vânătoare, 14 September 1944

Mirilă flew this aircraft on a low-level strafing raid on the main Axis air base of Szamosfalva (Someseni), near Kolozsvár (Cluj) on 14 September 1944. Following a single pass over the heavily-defended airfield, he returned to base and reported having set a 'large Gotha glider' (probably a Luftwaffe Go 242) on fire. Mirilă had already destroyed an I-16 and an unidentified Soviet reconnaissance aircraft on 27 June and 21 July 1941 respectively, as well as a B-24 on 22 July 1944, and the 'Gotha' would be his fourth, and last, victory. Note the pre-war red-yellow-blue cockades which replaced the pro-Axis Michael's cross national markings. The white fuselage band and wing tips were Allied identification symbols.

30
Bf 109G-6 'Yellow 3' Wk-Nr. 165560 of Locotenent aviator (Flying Officer) Tudor Greceanu, Grupul 9 vânătoare, late 1944

Greceanu flew this aircraft between 14 October and 14 December 1944, during which time he participated in the ARR's campaign against Axis forces. Note the improved vision Erla cockpit canopy and the tall fin and rudder, which

were introduced in the last G-6 production batch. Greceanu ended the war with 18 confirmed kills and at least five probables, although none of these were Axis aircraft. Note the emblem of Grupul 7 vânătoare on the engine cowling.

31
IAR 81C 'White 319' of Adjutant aviator (Corporal) Gheorghe Grecu, Escadrila 66 vânătoare, Grupul 2 vânătoare, Debrecen, Hungary, 9 February 1945

It was while flying this aircraft that Grecu shot down Rumanian Hs 129B-2 'White 214b', whose pilot was attempting to defect to the Germans. The ace was awarded the Order of the Red Banner for this controversial kill, which was ordered by the Soviets. Previously serving with Esc 49 vân, Gr 4 vân, Grecu had used IAR 81C 'White 394' to down two German transport aircraft (Me 323 Gigant '17' and Ju 52/3m '107') near Bucharest on 25 August 1944. These three aircraft represented seven of the eight victories attributed unofficially to Grecu.

32
Bf 109G-6 'Red 2' Wk-Nr. 166169 of Grupul 9 vânătoare, Lucenec (Losonc), February 1945

This aircraft is believed to have been the one in which top-ranking ARR ace Căpitan de rezervă aviator Constantin Cantacuzino, CO of Grupul 9 vânătoare, was shot down by a Bf 109G from JG 52 north-west of Detva, Slovakia, on 25 February 1945. A few minutes earlier he had claimed an Fw 190F destroyed, which represented his 54th, and final, kill to make him the top Rumanian ace of World War 2 with 69 ARR victorties.

(Back Cover)
IAR 81M 'White 104' of Sublocotenent aviator (Pilot Officer) Gheorghe Gulan, Grupul 1 vânătoare, Rosiori de Vede, spring 1944

Having previously served as a dive-bomber, this IAR 81 had been reassigned to the heavy fighter role following the fitment of two 20 mm Mauser cannon (hence the 'M' suffix) to combat American heavy bombers expected in the wake of Operation Tidal Wave. The three vertical stripes painted beneath the windscreen represent the ground victories that its pilot, Gheorghe Gulan, reportedly scored on the eastern front. He ended the war with two aerial kills – both B-24s (one shared) – which took his final tally to six aerial victories.

INDEX

Figures in **bold** refer to illustrations, plates are shown as plate number(s) with caption locators in brackets